TENNESSEE   GENEALOGICAL   RECORDS

HENRY   COUNTY

"OLD   TIME   STUFF "

Research, compiled and published

by

Edythe Rucker Whitley
Genealogist - Historian

( )( )( )( )( )

CLEARFIELD

Originally published
Nashville, Tennessee, 1968

Reprinted for
Clearfield Company, Inc. by
Genealogical Publishing Co., Inc.
Baltimore, Maryland
1991, 1998

International Standard Book Number: 0-8063-4797-X

Made in the United States of America

INTRODUCTION

* * * * * *

This book of Henry County abstracts is being presented to aid the genealogist and those interested in the pioneer families of the county.

May it serve as a MEMORIAL to those who settled there and built the thriving community which we find today.

The records of Henry County are rich in history; Some of them are fast crumbling from age.

This county has grown into one of the most popular recreational areas in the entire United States. It has become the South's most beautiful vacation land. Tennessee is a land of huge lakes, high mountains, beautiful rivers, fertile fields, rolling hills and modern towns and cities. Docks, cabins, parks, picnic areas, bathing beaches and many other facilities have been built for the convenience of vacationers who take advantage of the abundance of water, and sports found in Henry County. Kentucky Lake offers a wide range of recreational activity unsurpassed anywhere in the Mid-South.

It is the home of Paris Landing State Park.

Edythe Whitley.

* * * * * * * * * *

CONTENTS

* * *

* * *

HENRY COUNTY

* *

Let me tell you a little bit about Henry County, Tennessee. It was created by an Act of the General Assembly of the State of Tennessee, passed November 7, 1821, from the Western District. At the time of creation the boundaries were designated thus: "Beginning on the west bank of the Tennessee River, where the north boundary of the state leaves the same, running thence with the said boundary west to the second range line in the twelfth surveyor's district; thence South to a point two miles and a half south of the sixth sectional line in said district, thence east parallel with the said sectional line to the west boundary of Humphreys County; thence with said county line northwardly to the Tennessee River; thence down the said river with its various meanders to the beginning."

The county derived it's name from the Statesman Patrick Henry, and lies on the dividing ridge between the Tennessee and Mississippi Rivers. It is bounded on the north by the State of Kentucky, on the east by Stewart and Benton Counties, Tennessee, on the south by Carroll and on the west by Weakley County, Tennessee.

The central and southeastern portions of the county is drained principally by the Big Sandy River and its tributaries. Holly Fork and Bailey Fork drain the central portion of the county, and flow southwardly and empty into the West Sandy. The northeastern portion of the county below the mouth of Big Sandy River is drained by the Tennessee River and tributaries. Blood River is the main tributary.

The settlement of Henry County began about 1819. Joel and Willis T.Hagler, James Williams, Wm. Wyatt, Rev. Benjamin Peebles, Rev. John Manly, Richard and Hamilton F.Manly, John Stoddart, Abraham and William Waters, Cullen Bryant, Wm.Jones, James Hicks, Thomas T. Lilly, Johanan Smith, Henry Wall, the Randles, Reuben Bomar, Wm. Porter and his son (later known as Major Porter) all settled in the southeastern part about 1820.

Crawford Bradford, Araby Brown, Wm. Deloach, Thomas Gray and Hardy Mizell were among the first settlers in the northeastern part of the county.

John B.House came from Montgomery County to Henry County in 1819 and settled on the Obion near the famous mounds. On the North Fork of the Obion River are remarkable earth-works consisting of two large mounds about seventy and seventy-five feet in height, respectively, together with some smaller ones, and all surrounded with an earthen wall one mile in circumference from the point where it leaves the river to the place where it returns to it, only a short distance from the point of departure. When the county was first settled, this wall was from three to four feet in height, with elevated points at regular intervals about 100 feet apart, and between the two large mounds was a well which the early settlers called Jacob's Well.

The year following Houses settlement he returned to his old home and brought his family from Montgomery County.

Amos Milliken made a settlement on the Obion River in 1820. John Lawrence came and settled in the extreme northwest corner of the county. Josiah Cavitt settled on Terrapin Creek and Jesse Kuykendall and Jesse Paschall came about the same time.

Col. R.D. Caldwell and his father, James Caldwell, and Samuel Rogers were among the early and prominent settlers.

Adam Rowe settled on the head waters of the North Fork of the Obion before the county was organized; and was the first man married in the territory composing it. His marriage license being issued in Dover the County seat of Stewart County.

David Lemonds, father of one of the early County Court Clerks, settled on Town Creek. He afterward moved to Paris where he worked as a blacksmith as early as 1827.

John Maxwell, Daniel Ary, Henry Humphreys, Wm. Webb and Dr. Jacob Braswell, were also early pioneers. Dr. Braswell settled at a place known as "Naples", at which place he built a cabin so that a rock embedded in the earth formed the hearth to his fire-place.

In 1822 Lewis and Samuel McCorkle established themselves about seven miles southwest of Paris. James Greer, Alexander Harman, Col.Richard Porter, Hugh W.Dunlap, Daniel Culp (sometimes spelled Kulp), John Brown, and John Young were among the early settlers at Paris.

August 1822, brought David Searcy Greer and his father, James Grear, from Robertson County, Tennessee, bringing with them a stock of goods which they put up in a log cabin on the Middle Fork of the Obion River. This was the pioneer store of Henry County.

The influx of settlers can be learned from the fact that in 1830, only ten years after the settlement of the county was fully begun, its population was 12,249. In 1835 the Indian lands of North Mississippi came into market, and many of the early settlers were induced to emigrate to that State.

The first and most extensive land entries were made by locating land warrants granted by North Carolina to her soldiers for their services in the Revolutionary War and in the Indian Wars. These warrants were bought up by speculators, who obtained large tracts of the best lands of the county and later sold them to the actual settlers.

At one time John G. and Thomas Blount, neither of whom ever lived in the county, located land warrants covering 21,000 acres of the best lands of the county.

Landon Carter, of North Carolina, and the trustees of the University of North Carolina, obtained large tracts of land in the same manner.

Many of the actual settlers purchased land warrants before coming to the section. Very few of the soldiers to whom warrants were issued, ever obtained a home in Henry County, by locating them.

There were the "occupant entries" or entries of lands belonging to the Federal Government; of these lands Morgan Bricken, Daniel Campbell, Joseph Castlione, Philip Babb, James Howard, Littleton Allen, and Michael Embry made the first entries in the order here named.

The first water-power grist-mill in Henry County,was one mile northeast of Paris, and was erected about the year 1823 by Charles Crutchfield, and the next one was erected on Town Creek by a Mr. Lyons.About the year 1824, Jesse Kuykendall built a saw and grist-mill on the North Fork of the Obion River. Josiah Cavitt and sons, about the year 1835, built a grist-mill on Terrapin Creek.

Cotton was ginned in Henry County as early as 1824. The Chickasaw Cotton Mill, about two miles east of Paris was established about 1830. The Dinwiddie Cotton Factory, located about twelve miles southwest of Paris, was established after the Civil War. There yarn and cloth were manufactured. Oakley, White & Company, established a cotton factory near Paris about the year 1835.

It was around 1826 that William Waters raised the first tobacco in the county. Colonel R.D. Caldwell established a tobacco factory some fourteen miles northwest of Paris in 1846.

Henry County has always been extensive in agriculture and those activities which are associated with production from the earth and fertile soil.

In 1835 all that portion of Henry County lying east of Big Sandy River, was cut off and became a part of Benton County, which was then created from portions of Henry and Humphreys Counties, thus the Big Sandy and the Tennessee Rivers have formed the eastern boundary of Henry County.

The act which created Henry County provided that the court of pleas and quarter sessions for the new county should be held at the house of Henry Wall on the first Mondays of December, March, June and September of each year until otherwise provided by law. By an act passed November 16th, 1821 Sterling Brewer, James Fentress and Abram Maury were appointed commissioners for the County of Henry, to fix the place of the County seat.

Peyton Randle later resided at the Henry Wall place.

John Marberry, Esq., was elected chairman of the first court of Pleas and Quarter. The court then elected the following county officers viz - James G. Swisher, register; Thomas Gray, Sheriff: Henry Wall, ranger; Samuel McGowan, trustee; and Peter Liggin, coroner.

Constables were then appointed for each Captain's militia Company as follows - Amos H. Lacy, in Capt.Lacy's Company, and Alsey Elkins, in Capt. Grave's Company.

Henry Wall obtained a license to keep an ordinary at his house and gave bond.

Abner Johnson was permitted to keep a public ferry across Sandy River where he then resided, and also gave bond accordingly.

George House died in 1822 and the court appointed John House the administrator of the personal estate of the deceased at the March court. He was the first person appointed in the county of administer on an estate.

In June 1822 John Atkins was appointed constable in Capt. Brewer's Company, and Timothy Dalton constable in Capt. Reed's Company.

In December 1822 the court appointed Abner Pearce, James Leeper, John H. Randle, John Stoddart and James T. Williams commissioners to lay off and sell lots in the town to be established as the seat of Justice in the county and to superintend the building of a courthouse, prison, and stocks in the said town. At the same time James Jones, Dudley S.Jennings and Amos Milliken were appointed commissioners for the ensuing four years, to settle with the trustees and tax collectors.

The commissioners appointed to select the seat of Justice for the county, selected fifty acres where the town of Paris now stands. Of this fifty acres thirty seven and one half acres belonged to the estate of Joseph Blythe, and the balance to a tract entered by Peter Ruff. The town of Paris was laid

out by the commissioners in 1823, and had one hundred and
four lots, the public Square, streets and alleys as shown
in the original plat. Among those who purchased the first
lots were: James Greer, Samuel Hankins, and the Reverend
Samuel McGowan. Also, J.W. Looney, John Manly, Samuel
McCorkle, Daniel Culp (Kulp) and others. The first
courthouse was erected in 1820.

Paris has developed to be a thriving community,
and is the fourth to the largest city in the Western
District of the Volunteer State, and is one of the most
beautiful small cities in the South.

The town was named for Paris, France,in honor of
LaFayette who was visiting in Tennessee at the time the
name was chosen for the new seat of justice for the new
County of Henry. In 1950 the population of the city of
Paris and its immediate trade area was 28,667. Located
only sixteen miles from Kentucky Lake, largest of the TVA
chain of lakes, Paris is rapidly becoming one of the
vacation spots of the South. It has three city parks and
six playgrounds with supervised activities. Many stately
and beautiful homes grace the residential sections of Paris,
among them the antebellum home of a former Governor of
Tennessee, James D.Porter.

The old Minute Book of 1824-5 page 91, which is
available in the Courthouse at Paris, shows that it was
ordered by the court, that John Moore, Samuel Billingsley,
Elijah Hail, and others, be appointed a jury to view and
lay out and mark a road of the third class from Liggins
bridge to Hoover's saw-mill, the nearest and best way.
Issued by the court 23 September 1824.

The court of 4 October 1825 ordered Nathaniel Hale,
Nicholas Hale, be hands on the road from the fork road near
Taylor's three and one half miles west. Thomas Taylor was
the overseer. (Min. 1824-5 p.320).

December 12th, 1825 it was ordered by the court that
Solomon Patton, James Tart, Danl. Hansberry, Wade Barton,
William Hopkins be a jury to view and lay off a road leaving
the iron banks road between McGowan and Hobbs field to the
State line (meaning of course Kentucky) and in the direction
to town of Mayfield in Kentucky (Court Min. 1825-28 p.10).

The sub-division of the county into Civil Districts
came in 1826. The commissioners appointed for this purpose
were - W.S. Patterson, Contantine Frazier, Crawford Bradford,
James C.Gainer and Michael Brooks. In 1850 the districts
were re-organized and increased to twenty, there having been
only seventeen at first. In 1870 they were increased to
twenty-five. Since that time various other changes have been
made to keep up with the growth of the county.

William Arnold was the first solicitor general.

In the year 1824 the justices of the peace were: Jacob Hoover, Samuel Wynn, Spearman Holland, John H. Crutcher, Peter Liggin, John Horton, John Stoddart, Kenneth Reddick, John A Newland, Rev.Benjamin Peeples (also spelled Peebles, and Peobles), William Ward and Bryan Bunch.

The first will probated in the county was that of Thomas Wilson, deceased, in June 1823.

In March 1823 John Boyd obtained a license to keep an ordinary in the town of Paris, and William Massey and Joel Robertson were granted the same priviledge, and in December 1824 Wm. Wyatt obtained a license " to keep a public ferry across Sandy River at his landing above Wyatt's mill". William Holt was given permission to build a dam across Middle Fork of Obion River. At the next term of court David Davis obtained a license to keep a frerry across Sandy River at his landing, and James B. Quigley and Jesse C. Gainer each obtained permission to keep an ordinary at his residence. In 1826 Obediah B.Smith and Hugh W. Dunlap each obtained permission to keep an ordinary at his house in the town of Paris. In 1859 the Old Paris Inn also known as the Daniel House, located on the Southwest corner of the Public Square changed it's name to the Yowell House and James A.Yowell became the new proprietor. In 1857 the Union Hotel at Paris was operated by S.B.McCutchen.

It was about 1856 that Rev.Benjamin Peeples was elected County Judge by a vote of the people. After one year the law was repealed.

The first term of the Circuit court of Henry County was held at the house of Henry Wall in October 1822, with the Honorable Joshua Haskill, judge presiding. Joshua Haskell came to Tennessee from Rhode Island and settled at Murfreesboro, in Rutherford County, having served previously in the Creek War. He was a lawyer and in 1821 was appointed Judge of the newly-created Eighth Circuit, and removed to Jackson, in Madison County, so as to reside within his circuit. In 1829 he was impeached,but was acquitted for want of a constitutional majority against him, the vote being a tie. Joshua W.Caldwell in "Sketches of the Bench and Bar" page 237 "There seems to be no room to doubt that Judge Haskell's judicial habits were, to say the least, somewhat informal. Nevertheless he was very popular and held the office until 1836, serving in all fifteen years." He was the father of William T.Haskell, a poet, an orator, a converser, a dreamer. William T.Haskell is numbered among those most prominent early Tennesseans.

The Circuit Court of Henry County suspended business during the war period from September 1861 to September 1865. On December 1, 1882 Shim Forrest, of Henry County, killed his grandfather, David Cruise, and his own mother, Mrs. Jane Forrest. He was tried in the Circuit Court at the May term 1883 and sentenced to be hanged August 3rd following. He took an appeal to the Supreme Court where the decision of the lower court was affirmed; On July 11, 1884 the death penalty was carried out.

The Judges of the Circuit Court have been Joshua Haskell, 1822-24 already referred to; John C. Hamilton 1824-32; John W. Cook 1832-36; Wm.R.Harris 1836-1846; William Fitzgerald 1846 to September 1861; Lucien L.Hawkins 1865-70; James D.Porter 1870-74; Joseph R.Hawkins 1874-78; Samuel B.Ayers 1878-79; Clinton Aden 1879-86; and W. H. Swiggart 1866 etc.

Of those mentioned above, William R.Harris, was an elder brother of Isham G.Harris, and was born in Montgomery County, North Carolina, September 26, 1803, and was killed by the explosion of the steamboat "Pennsylvania" on the Mississippi River, near Memphis, January 13, 1858. While he was a child his father moved to Bedford County, Tennessee, and then to Franklin County. At one time William R.Harris was Deputy Sheriff of Franklin County, and while he held that office, studied at night and kept up with a class in Carrick Academy. He began to read law in 1825, and was admitted to the bar in 1827. Settling in Paris, Henry County, soon after the establishment of the county, he secured an excellent practice and rose rapidly in the profession. In 1836 he was appointed by Governor Cannon to fill a vacancy created by the resignation of the Judge of the Ninth Circuit. This office he held until 1845, when he returned to the bar. In 1851 he removed to Memphis. He succeeded Judge Turley as Judge of the Common Law and Chancery Court of Memphis, by appointment , and was afterwards elected. His prominence spread throughout the South.

The Weekly Register, newspaper, published in Paris, Saturday May 6, 1848 E.G.Atkins , proprietor, advertised for sale for taxes which sale was issued by the Circuit Court, and which sale was to take place January 20, 1848 under the direction of Thomas Dodd, collector of Public Tax for 1847, and reports the following tracts of land, town lots and parts of town lots as having been given for tax thereon due and unpair: Giles Cooke,heirs 4 acres Civil District No.1; David Coleman, 180 acres, Civil District No.3; Joshua Glover's heirs, 56 acres, Civil District No.4 ; Joseph H. Little 100 acres in Civil District No.4;James Park 100 acres in Civil District No.7; Jonathan Hampton,heirs, 1000 acres in Civil District No.15; Mary Ann Christian 97 acres in Civil District No.15.

The same newspaper, with J.A. Banister as printed, and the same date of issue as above, shows the new subscribers to be --- G.W.Cos, John L.McConnell, R.D. Caldwell, Robert Lemmons, Abraham Martin, Wiley Price, Gova Cox,Asa Cox,Senr., Asa Cox, Junr., Jno.B.McGehee, I.L. Alexander, John Bragg,

Wm.H. Haynes, and James W.Ray.

The first term of the Chancery Court of Henry County was held in the Courthouse at Paris, beginning on the first Monday of June 1846 with Andrew McCampbell, Chancellor, presiding, and Eldridge G.Atkins, clerk and Master. Chancellor McCampbell was of a Scotch-Irish family which still has many representatives in Tennessee, especially in Knox and Jefferson Counties. He was born in Rockbridge County,Virginia, May 8, 1797. While he was an infant his father died, and soon afterwards the family moved to Knox County, in East Tennessee settling about five miles East of Knoxville. The mother's maiden name was Anderson, and she was the aunt of Samuel, Robert, William E., and Isaac Anderson. Andrew McCampbell read law under the direction of his brother, John A.McCampbell, who was a prominent member of the Knoxville bar. Andrew did not practice at Knoxville, however, but in 1819 removed to Jackson, Tennessee, where he remained for about one year, and then went to Paris, Tennessee. In 1839 he was elected Chancellor for West Tennessee, in which capacity he served till 1847, and then retired. He resumed the practice of law and continued in it until his death, which occurred January 4, 1884. Governor Porter's eugoly of Chancellor McCampbell may be found in "Bench and Bar" by Joshua Caldwell, page 253.

The Chancery Court of Henry County also suspended operation of business from January 1862 to September 1866, due to the "War of the Rebellion" (Civil War). In addition to Chancellor McCampbell, some of the other early Chancellors have been - Calvin Jones 1847-54; Isaac B.Williams 1854-1860; John Somers 1866-86; Albert G.Hawkins 1886, etc.

In September 1857 the Chancery Court at Paris, by the Clerk and Master B.C. Brown offered for sale 66 54/160 acres of land in Range 5, Section 16, on Clark's River adjoining the Kentucky line, as decreed in suit of George T. Shearman VS Susan Frails et als. (Paris newspaper 1857).

Paris and Henry County have always had an excellent supply of members of the bar. In 1824 such names a William Fitzgerald, Hugh W.Dunlap, J.W.Cook, B.Gillespie, M.A. Martin, William Arnold, appear. In 1848 Charles B. Darwin and E.C. Atkins advertised as practicing attorneys in Paris. In 1859 the old newspapers show A.P. Greer, James S.Brown, B.F.Lamb, J.J.Lamb, Dunlap & Porter, Aden & Crawford, J.W. Thomason, and John W.Harris had their singles in the wind. They advertised in the Paris Weekly Sentinel of August 12, H.F.Cummins, editor and proprietor.

Two watchmakers and jewlers did their share of advertising in 1857. W.W.Bowman and F.M. Cheek, both in Paris. In 1848 John. R.McCall a dentist with office in Paris, was seeking to practice.

It should be here mentioned that in 1857 The Paris Male

Academy had as principal, the Rev.E.C. Trimble. At the
same time Edward Cooper, was President of the Odd Fel-
low's Female College at Paris.

During the Florida War, Captain Wm.N.Porter raised
a company of soldiers in Henry County and took them to
Fayetteville, Tennessee, where he learned that their services
were not needed, and then returned home.

At the outbreak of the Mexican War, Captain Preston
G.Haynes raised a Company in the county, which joined the
United States Army and served through that war.

Daniel L. Futrell, a native of North Carolina, born
in Northampton County on the Roanoke River, April 24, 1792,
died September 17, 1857. He moved to Kentucky in 1812. He
was a soldier in the Indian War. He was in the battle of
Taledeago and Horseshoe Bend under General Jackson. He was
also in the battle of New Orleans. After peace was declared
he returned to Kentucky; Married on the 24th of December
1816 and in February 1824 migrated to Henry County, Tennessee. His death was reported in The Paris Sentinel of
Spetmeber 25, 1857, Hiram F.Cummins, published.

Henry County, like other parts of the country had her
share of pensioned veterans from the Revolutionary War.
Among those who drew pensions from Henry County prior to
1840 - Lewis Atkins, pensioned in 1832 age 77 had served
in North Carolina; William Bonner, age 78, who served in the
North Carolina militia drew pension in 1832; Elias Bowden
age 72 applied for pension and drew for having rendered
service in the Virginia line; William Buntin, did not
show in the 1832 list but was on the rolls of 1840 age 73
years; Charles Byles, age 85 appears on the 1832 list and
served in the North Carolina line; Alexander Craig, is shown
in the 1832 list as age 76, served in the North Carolina line.
He was still living in 1840; Joshua Denkins, age 72 was
listed in 1832 as having served from North Carolina; Thomas
Frazier was placed on the pension list by 1818 age 73, having
served in North Carolina. He was transferred from Cumberland
County,North Carolina to Henry County, Tenn, In 1840 he was
living in Gibson County, Tennessee.

George Brittain, was on the pension list of 1818 at
which time he was residing in Smith County, Tennessee age 94;
in 1840 he was living in Henry County. He served in the
North Carolina line.

John Graham , age 69 from North Carolina, and James
Haynes ,age 74 from Virginia were listed in 1832.

John Hearn, age 77 years from South Carolina; Edward
Hogan , age 72, from North Carolina; David Hutcheson, age
79, from North Carolina; John Jackson age 69 from Virginia;

Obadiah Jackson, age 75, from North Carolina; David Jones, age 69, from Virginia; William Matheny, age 77 from North Carolina, all show on the list of pensiones for the Revolution and the War or 1812.

William McGowan, age 78, from South Carolina; Martin Neace, age 82; John Palmer, age 78 from Georgia, were on the list in 1832. John Palmer's widow drew pension in 1840 and was then living with John L.Palmer.

William Potts, age 68 from South Carolina; Robert Ramsey,age 75, from North Carolina; Samuel Rogers, age 71 from North Carolina; John Smith, age 71, fron North Carolina; James Walker (pensioned 1828 War 1812); Thomas C. Wills, age 69 from Maryland; Joseph Witherington, age 75 from North Carolina: John Wollard,age 74 from Virginia; and William Young , age 72 from North Carolina, all appear on the list for Henry County in 1832 except those mentioned as exceptions.

Then came the Civil War or the "War of the Rebellion" which is also referred to as the "War Between the States". The first company raised in Henry County for the Confederate Army was that of Captain Edward Fitzgerald, in April of 1861 and they joined the One Hundred and Fifty-fourth Tennessee Regiment organized in Memphis. Other companies were raised by Captains B.B. Bunch, M.Long, T.H. Conway, J.D. Dumas, J.H. Porter, J. E. Fowler, W.D. Hallum, H.W. Ballard, A.W. Cardwell, which were mustered into the Fifth Confederate Infantry on May 20, 1861.

The Forty-sixth Tennessee Confederate Infantry was all raised in Henry County with few exceptions.

Four cavalry companies were organized in the county, commanded by Captains J.G. Stocks, T.H. Taylor, M.H. Freeman, and Cardwell Wilson, all of which served under General Forrest.

Captain Edward Arbuckle raised a company in Henry County which served in the Federal Army.

General Felix H.Zollicoffer at the age of seventeen, in company with two others, all young men, commenced the publication of a newspaper in 1829 or 1830, in the town of Paris. Their venture was not long to live however.

William Gates published a paper in Paris during the thirties.

S. B. Aden, in the forties, published a paper in Henry County. It was still active in 1852. In 1855 the Sentinel was established by H.F. Cummins and operated a few years. The Analysis was published for some time prior to the War of '65, by Dr. Darwin.

A paper called THE BEE was published by John W. Cook. Another called The INTELLIGENCER was established 1866 by H.W. Wall and W B.Porter. Then came THE GAZETTE in 1877 by Aolsapple and Hutchens. It changed hands several times and in 1879 the name was changed to PARIS POST.

In 1883 the Intelligencer and the POST were consolidated under the name of PARIS POST-INTELLIGENCER which was edited by Squire J.R. Rison.

The PARIS TRIBUNE came along about 1886 and was published and edited by James P.McGee and Headley Boyd.

There were seventeen postoffices in Henry County, in 1857, namely (with the postmaster) - Albany, with John Dillahunty; Barren Hill, with James Walker; Caledonia, with William M.Maxwell; Chanceford, with Thomas Poyner; Cheap Valley, with James A.Nance; Como,with Samuel S.Boss; Conyersville, with Henry P. Barbee; Cottage Grove, with John W. Todd; Ell Grove, with Vincent B.Walker; Manlyville, with William C.Manly; Mansfield, with Wm.H.Thompson; Mount Holyoke, with James Cowan; Mouth of Sandy, with John Cooney, Jr; New Boston, with Benjamin T. Bowden; North Fork, with William F. England; Paris, with William C.Williams; and Sandy Hill, with John H. Warren.

Cottage Grove was in the northwest part of the county, and was established about 1845 on lands belonging to Dr. Bowden.

Conyersville was in the northern part of the county, established about 1846 on lands belonging to Pack. Conyer. In 1857 John W. Carter had a farm one mile west of Conyersville, and the Conyersville Inn was under new management. Sandy Edmunds was the new proprietor. John Curd had been the former operator and proprietor.

Henry Station on the Louisville and Nashville Railroad in the southwest part of the county was not established until about 1858 on lands of Peterson and Busby.

Como near the west line of the county was established about 1859 according to most historians, but it was already a postoffice in 1857.

Elkhorn, another community with some settlement, was nine miles east of Paris.

Buchanan, established during the administration of President Buchanan, was in the northeast part of the county.

Manlyville was established on the lands of William Manly. Caledonia was in the southwestern part of the county.

James Johnson, Senior, lived on Iron Banks Road, twelve miles southwest of Paris in Civil District No.12, in 1848. Henry Trevathan, in 1848, lived one mile south of Paris on the Huntingdon Stage Road. Terrence Cooney, had his place of business in the 15th Civil District at the Mouth of Sandy.

Thomas Diggs lived in Civil District No. 5. about seven miles southwest of Paris in 1848.

The Methodist Episcopal, the Baptist and the Cumberland Presbyterians were pioneer churches in the county. The pioneer Methodist ministers were Benjamin Peebles and John Manly; Also Rev.Couch and Samuel Sankins. Rev.Benjamin Peeples was the first minister sent into West Tennessee west of the Tennessee River in the capacity of a minister. In 1819 he was a minister in Carroll County, Tennessee.

The pioneer Baptist ministers in Henry County were - Rev.Trainer, Lewis Baldwin, Samuel McGowan, Jacob Browning, James Conyers, James Haynes, and Lewis M.Edgar.

The Cumberland Presbyterian Ministers who arrived in the county quite early were- William Henry, James Laws, Robert Baker, James Mackey and Richard Beard.

Of the early families, the Lovelaces came from Halifax County,Virginia. The McNeills were from Carroll County to Henry but were originally from North Carolina. The Mathis family came from Kentucky to Henry County, Tennessee.

Benjamin J. Barton, a native of Kentucky, born 1798, came to this county about 1824 and died around 1830. He married Rebecca Killebrew, also born in Kentucky in 1800 and lived to 1875. They had a son J.Wade Barton who was born in the 11th District of Henry County. J. Wade Barton married September 17, 1846 Mary Ann Hardy of Kentucky.

John and Sarah (Manly) Atkins came from Anson County, North Carolina to Montgomery County, Tennessee, then to Stewart County and in 1823 to Henry County. She died 1827 and he in 1847. They were Methodist . Their son Hon. J.D.C. Atkins was born near Paris, June 4, 1825. He graduated from East Tennessee University in 1846. Read law, and in 1849 entered the Legislature and was re-elected in 1851. In 1855 elected to the State Senate. He went to Congress in 1857 and was defeated when running for re-election in 1859. He was elected Lieutenant-Colonel of the Fifth Tennessee Confederate States Army, May 20, 1861. He was elected to provinsional Confederate Congress, and in 1867 with two other gentlemen founded the Paris Intelligencer which he edited for some years. In the year 1847 he married Miss Elizabeth Porter, daughter of Col. Wm.Porter, a prominent citizen of Henry County. To them were born five children : Sarah (Mrs. Hugh P.Dunlap), Bettie (Mrs. ProfF.H. Hunter), John D., Mattie, Clintie (Mrs. Dudley Porter). This family has been one of the most progressive and outstanding in the county.

1840 SOLDIER PENSION LIST

* * * *

Elias Bowden, age 77 years, living with Elias Bowden.

Daniel Rogers, age 72 years, living with Daniel Rogers.

Alexander Craig, age 85 years, living with Alexander Craig.

Polly Simmons, age 74 years, (widow of Veteran) living with James P.Simmons.

Susanna Palmer, age 77 years, (widow), living with John L. Palmer.

Matthew Alexander, age 85 years, living with Matthew Alexander.

William Powel, age 74 years, living with William Powel.

Joseph Weatherington, age 82 years, living with Joseph Weatherington.

Matthew Myrick, age 88 years, living with William Myrick.

James Haynes, age 79 years, living with James Haynes.

Martin Neace, Senior, age 82 years, living with Martin Neace, Senior.

William Bunton, age 73 years, living with William Bunton.

Robert Ramsey, age 82 years, living with Robert Ramsey.

Britton George, age 102 years, living with Britton George.

==

Dots and Dashes.

Dr. Marion Alexander born in South Carolina, physician and surgeon, married Delilah Crutchfield, born in North Carolina, died about 1878 age about 49 years. About 1842 Dr. Alexander went to sea and never was heard of again. His son D.F. Alexander remained with his mother until about twenty years of age, then went to Salisbury, Tennessee, to work in a Dry Goods store. When the war broke out he enlisted in the Confederate Army, May 20,1861, Company F, Fifth Regiment Tennessee Infantry, Was elected Sergeant. Became Captain. In December 1865 D.F. Alexander married Nellie Wright a native of Paris, Tennessee.

The Rowe family of Henry County, Tenn. came from Muhlenburg County, Kentucky.

1883 -----PENSIONERS ----

(U.S. Senate Reports --- 47th Congress 2nd Series , Executive
Document No.84. Published 1883 part 5. Federal Pensioners
(Soldiers).

142395 Teresa Kimbret, postoffice Como, Henry County, Tennessee,
widow, placed on pension April 1870.

128826 Mary J.Baughman, postoffice Como, Henry County, Tennessee,
widow, placed on pension rolls May 1869.

145319 Sarah V. Tate, postoffice, Como, Henry County, Tennessee,
widow, placed on pension rolls October 1870.

15853 Susanna P.Conner, Postoffice Como, Henry County, Tennessee,
widow of 1812, placed on pension rolls January 1879.

25533 Mary Duncan, postoffice Conyersville, Henry County, Tennessee,
widow of war of 1812, Placed on pension rolls July 1879.

28727 Louisa Jones, postoffice Conyersville, Henry County, Tennessee, Widow of War of 1812, Places on pension rolls February
1880.

32335 Lavinia Valentine, postoffice Conyersville, Henry County,
Tennessee, Widow of War 1812, Placed on Pension rolls 1882.

12405 Wm.N. Willis, Postoffice Conyersville, Henry County, Tennessee, Served in the War of 1812. Placed on pension rolls Feb.
1872.

18545 Charity Ann Powell, Postoffice Cottage Grove, Henry County,
Tennessee, widow of War of 1812, Placed on pension roll Feb.1879.

24714 Hannah Lee, Postoffice Elkhorn, Henry County, Tennessee,
widow of soldier of War of 1812. Placed on pension roll Jany.
1879.

19256 Rosannah Barfield, postoffice Haylerville, Henry County,
Tennessee, widow of soldier of War of 1812. Placed on pension
roll Feby.1879.

92072 Margaret A. Hair, Postoffice Henry, Henry County, Tennesse,
widow. Placed on pension roll April 1867.

176487 Nancy H. Blacknall, Postoffice Henry, Henry County, Tennessee, widow, Placed on pension roll Feby 1877.

119963 Eliz!th Anglin, Postoffice Henry, Henry County, Tennessee, widow. Placed on pension roll October 1868.

116893 Mary A. Green, Postoffice Manleyville, Henry County,Tenn-
essee, widow, Placed on pension roll March 1869.

24889 Elizth H.Rainey, Postoffice, Paris, Henry County, Tennessee,widow of soldier of War of 1812, Placed on pension roll June 1879.

21512 Mary Beard, postoffice Paris, Henry County, Tennessee, widow of war of 1812, placed on pension roll March 1879.

15875 John Pierce, Postoffice Paris, Henry County, Tennessee, Served in the War of 1812. Placed on pension roll April 1872.

14699 Adam Rowe, postoffice Paris, Henry County, Tennessee, Served in the War of 1812. Placed on pension roll March 1872.

189491 Judy (alias) Wright, Postoffice Paris,Henry County, Tennessee. widow. Placed on pension roll August 1880. Given also as Judy Moore.

150418 Malinda C.Taylor, Postoffice, Paris, Henry County, Tennessee, widow, Placed on pension roll May 1871

9900 William Dunn, postoffice, Paris, Henry County, Tennessee. Served in the War of 1812. Placed on pension roll December 1871

6025 Bartlett Hinchey, postoffice Paris, Tennessee, Henry County. Served in the War of 1812. Pensioned October 1871.

9088 John Hart, postoffice Paris, Tennessee, Henry County, served in the War of 1812. Pensioned December 1871.

14957 Joel Hagler, postoffice Paris, Henry County, Tennessee. Pensioned April 1872.

25130 Frances Long, postoffice Paris, Henry County, Tennessee. Widow of soldier of War of 1812. Placed on pension rolls June 1879.

28056 Mary Martin, postoffice Paris, Henry County, Tennessee, widow of soldier of War of 1812. Placed on pension roll December 1879.

19246 Penina Marro, postoffice Paris, Henry County, Tennessee. Placed on pension roll Feby 1879

117864 Susan J. Atkins, postoffice Paris, Henry County, Tennessee, widow. Placed on pension August 1868.

28857 Delilah Stennet, postoffice Paris, Henry County, Tennessee, Widow of soldier of War of 1812. Placed on pension roll. Feby. 1880.

18287 Lucinda Foster, postoffice Paris Landing, Henry County,
Tennessee. Placed on pension roll February 1879.

5825 Elizth Morton, postoffice Paris Landing, Henry County,
Tennessee.Placed on pension roll January 1874.

182309 Jane S.Korregay. postoffice Springdale, Henry County,
Tennessee. Mother of a soldier. Placed on pension roll
October 1878.

==

DOTS AND DASHES OF TENNESSEE.

Just north of Paris, on the Puryear road, is a house
whose very appearance points to a history of rich family life.
It is a two story which was at the time this notation was made
by William Hopkins. A family of six moved there shortly after
the Civil War, three girls, three boys, children of Fotzgerald
Williams, a Congressman from this district who served in the
cabinet of a fiery Tennessean named Andrew Jackson. None of the
six ever married. Mrs. Charles Watkins,one of the few sur-
vivors of the Williams clan, recalled that though Isaac Williams never left his front yard he was a man of importance in
the community. Fitzgerald, the older practiced law in a little
log cabin near the house. He was one of the first lawyers of
Paris. (MSS. Tenn.State Library, Filed under Henry Co.Tenn.)

In 1823 William Young, wife and eight children with
seven slaves started from Barren County,Kentucky to Henry
County, Tennessee, with one ox wagon to haul their belongings
and several horses and cattle. Newton Young the younger of the
eight children was born Nov. 30, 1814. Young's plantation was
a province within itself. At the grandmother's sale in 1888
there was sold over 100 yards of home made geans which went
fast at $10.00 for strips of 10 yards.

George F.Diggs died at the age of 93 years in May
1932. The Paris Post Intelligence of May 19 had this to say -
George F.Diggs, leading farmer and largest land owner. His
parents settled in the county in 1822. George Fletcher Diggs
93 pioneer of Henry County, died at home on South Dunlap
Street. He was the son of John H. and Sarah (Webb) Diggs,
and was born July 1, 1839. The family settled near Palestine
Church. On January 10,1861 G.F.Diggs married Angeline Upchurch
and they had four daughters. Two survive ,Mrs. Byron Looney,
and Mrs. James Freeman. Mrs. Diggs died fourteen years before
her husband.

Paris Post Intelligencier, June 28,1929. Rev.Samuel
Williams Hankins, lived in 1800 and helped establish the history
of the county. He died 1846 and buried in Memphis.

INDEX WILL BOOK # 1. 1879-1902

==

Dots and Dashes .

The Trevathan family came from North Carolina to
Henry County, Tennessee.

The Todd family were from Wake County,North Carolina
to this county.

The Thomason family came from North Carolina. The
Lyles also came from North Carolina. The Wade family came
from Randolph County,North Carolina or that vicinity.
The Weldon family came to Henry County, Tennessee from
Franklin County,North Carolina. The Wynns also came from
North Carolina.

HENRY COUNTY WILL ABSTRACTS.

* * * *

John Swift,will, names wife Mary Swift. Sons Garland
Swift and Richard Swift. Tract of land I now live on, 150 acres
purchased of Joseph Looney. Daughter Virginia Louisa Swift.
Children: Arthur Swift, James Swift, Ann Winn, Marietta Waters.
Harriett Swift. Emana Swift. Garland and Arthur Swift act as
guardian of said children not of age. Dated January 26, 1838.
Signed John Swift. Witnessed by John Barfield. Garland Swift.
(Henry Co.Wills 1838-41 p.1).

William L.Dillahunty received from James Dillahunty
and John Haynes administrators of William Dillahunty decd, $64
10/13 a part of share of estate of William Dillahunty. Feby 13,
1830. Signed William S.Dillahunty. John Dillahunty and Luzana
Dillahunty. (Henry Co.Wills 1838-41 p.40). Louzana Dillahunty
widow guardian for eight minor heirs to wit- Green Charlott,
Frances, Joseph , Oliver, Rachael , Louzana, Tabitha Dillahunty
receipt for their share.

Charles Biles will. Son Stephen Biles a negro slave.
Son Michael Biles to have a negro slave. Daughter Polly Alderson
To Johnson M.Walker when of age certain property. Grandsons-
Joseph Pearson, Thomas Lincoln, John Wiley Biles. Granddaughters
Fanny S.Alexander, Elizabeth C.Biles. Will dated 26 Oct. 1837.
Signed Charles (x) Biles. Witnesses, Joseph H.B.Wilson and
John J. Erwin. (Wills 1838-41 p.44).

William Whitfield's will. Sons Lewis and George Whitfield land. Land Lewis Whitfield now lives on. Son John Whitfield land. Young son Needam, Son William, Son Bryant, son
James. My daughters. not by name. James Lee senior and my wife
Hannah Whitfield executors. Dated May 14, 1839. (Wills 1838-41
page 51).

Thomas Griffin's Will. Wife Mary to be executor (Executrix). Son James Griffin. Son Daniel Griffin. Son William N.
Griffin. Daughter Emily wife of David Cofman. Daughter Louviana
widow of Geo.W. Ranken. Daughter Ellenor wife of William R.Lewis
(or Lawes ?). Daughter Mary Griffin. Daughter Malinda Griffin.
Daughter Caroline Griffin. Dated April 22, 1829. (Wills 1838-41
page 69).

Will of Isaac Akers deceased. Wife Lucinda land and
etc. Divide property between Benjamin, Isaac, Lucinda, Uriah
and Abner Akers. Divide the land. Son William. Son Thomas.
Appoints wife Lucinda Akers executrix. Dated 18 October 1839.
Signed Isaac Akers. Witnesses by Willie H.Burch, Jo.W.Muzzale.
Feb.3, 1840. (Wills 1838-41 p.95.)

Woodward Daniels' Will. Daughter Lutrecy Baker. Son
John Daniel. Daughter Milicent Daniel. Appoints son John and
Ephraim C.Baker executors. Dated 10 March 1840.(Wills 1838-41
page 107).

Michael Biles left will dated Feby, 6, 1840,made. Wife Nancy W. Biles. Daughter Catherine F.; Daughter Mary M.; Daughter Nancy Jane; Daughter Margaret E.; -- and Daughter Lucietia T. ; Son Thomas L.Biles. Son John W.Biles. (Wills 1838-41 p.108).

Joseph Peters will. Refers to "my brother and partner in the Mills and Cotton factory". Jeremy Peters all of the estate. Nephew Henry Peters Gray son of David Gray Jr. of Andover, Mass.; Uncle Arice Peters of Massachusetts and sister in law Johanna wife of Jeremy Peters. Will dated 19 July 1839. Signed Joseph Peters. (Wills 1838-41 p.118).

From will book 1828-32 page 47. Francis Blair gave acknowledgement to receipt of money for sale of a slave named Peter in Henry County. Dated January 2, 1826.This was acknowledged in Cape Geradeau. Missouri.

Nuncupative will of Mathew Anderson, deceased, provides to sell land and pay debts. dated 23 Oct. 1829. (Wills 1828-32 p.48 (51)).

The will of Buris Eastis, 6 August 1829. Wife Martha to have house I live in and 90 acres of and and household goods. Son John. My daughters, not by name. Grandson William Green. Daughter Dicey and Daughter Delilia. Son Thomas. Son Burris. Land on Big Harpeth River. Thomas Estis executor. (Wills 1828-32 p 61 (58)).

The will of Asa Atkins, dated March 24, 1830. Names wife Winyford Atkins to have land. Refers to "My children". Given Nancy Polly Alfred and Hampton already. My children, Nancy Polly Alfred Hampton, Martha Lucy, Betsy. (The names written without having comma separating the names). (Wills 1828-32 page 75.).

The will of James Carter, 25 April 1828. Wife Delilia land I live on. Land adjoining Organ Thomas's Mill pond. Daughter Sarah to have certain land. To son James Terry Carter certain land. Son Jerome Carter. Daughter Eliza Carter. Daughter Agnes Carter. Daughter Martha Carter. Daughter Rebecca Carter. Son Isham Carter. (Wills 1828-32 page 85.)

The will of James Stem. August 1, 1830. Wife Sarah property for live. My children to receive equally in the division. Not named. Appoints friend Richard Wright, Leonard Bullock, James Oglivil, and James Moore as the executors. (Wills 1828-32 p. 86).

John Boothe left will. Recorded 26 May 1826. In it he refers to plantation and etc. Support for wife Martha Ann and children. Son Zachariah Boothe. Son Lemuel. Son John Westley Boothe. Daughter Mary Jenkins. Daughter Sarah Boothe, Son Tapley Boothe. Daughter Tabitha Boothe. Son

William D.Boothe. Daughter Martha Ann Boothe. Dated 16 Aug.
1826. Signed John (X) Boothe . Appointed son Lemuel as the
executor. Witnessed by Stephen Nance. Young B.Nekins. (Wills
1828-32 p.15.)

  The will of Jesse Snipes deceased names wife Mary to
have plantation I live on . The children to be supported.
two sons and three daughters not of age. Elisa James Harvey
Lucinda Catherine Mary Jane Also William Snipes. Appoints
Marey Snipes and James Miller executors. dated 6 July 1827.
(Wills 1828-32 page 40.).

  Thomas Reavis left will in which he names his wife
Elizabeth to have certain property for life. Then he names
"My heirs" ---John M. Reavis, Samuel B.Reavis, Thomas C.
Reavis, Lewis W.Reavis. Henry W.Reavis, Lucy A.J. Reavis,
Margaret Reavis, Elizabeth G.Reavis, James B.Reavis, and
William F.Reavis. Appoints Samuel B.Reavis and John Manley
and Col. William Porter Jr. as executors. Margaret, James,
Elizabeth and William are to be schooled. The will bears
date May 18, 1829. (Wills 1828-32 p.41.).

  The will of Thomas Flippin is recorded in which he
devises to Thomas Neal and Nancy his wife, certain land. To
James Flippin certain land; To Isaac Flippin certain land;
To John Flippin or his heirs certain property. To Elizabeth
Goodman wife of George Goodman or their heirs certain property. To Mary Goodall wife of Lodowick Goodall decd, or
heirs certain property. To Thomas H.Flippin and his heirs.
To the children of Jesse Goodman by his first wife Rhoda
Goodman deceased. To Allen Flippin or his heirs certain
property. To Jesse Flippin. Appoints Thomas H. Flippin
and Allen executors. (Wills 1828-32 p.87).

  James Allen left will dated 21 August 1830, in
which he calls for daughter Isabella Allen. "Mychildren"-
William Allen, Isabella Allen, Margaret Allen, Samuel B.Allen,
Benjamin Allen. Beckey Allen, and grandson William Allen (if
he remain with the family until of age). Appoints Amos
Milliken and William Allen and Samuel Allen as executors.
The last two being sons. (Wills 1828-32 p.105).

  William Stone's will was recorded January 14,1831
In it he names wife Elizabeth to have land whereon I now
reside, 600 acres etc. Names his children. John Stone,
Nancy Williams, Jonathan Stone, Ebenezer Stone, Betsey Ann
Stone, Chlacy Jane Stone and William L.Stone. (Wills 1828-
1832 p.106).

  The will of David Gray provides " My plantation"
be kept until my oldest son Thomas Gray becomes of age. Wife
Eliza. My children. Son Thomas. Daughter Armenta Gray. Appoints Crawford Bradford,David C.Cowan and James Gray as
executors. 4 May 1831 (Wills 1828-32 p.134).

The will of William Porter wife Agnes Porter, to
whom he left property. William Porter Jr. mentioned. All
of heirs not of age. To George and Sarah Wilson $978.70
To Thomas K.Porter and to James D.Porter a similar
amount. To **David** Wilson, Eliza his wife and to Benjamin R.Maclin. etc. (Wills 1832-34 p.37). Wife Agnes
if she remain a widow 360 acres of land, household furniture
and Kitchen furniture. He divided his slaves. There were
a number of them. My daughters Mary H.Porter and Rebecca
W Porter to learn to Read and write, arithmetic and
through the Rule of three and provides for them until
they are of age. He had given his son William Porter,Jr
one hundred and forty acres of land where he now lives.
Refers to land in Port Williams Kentucky. To Thomas and
Diannah K.White one hundred and fifty two dollars, six
cents. I have already given them. He refers to his account
book which he called " my private entry book". I have
delivered Benjamin R.Maclin and his wife Malinder now
Malinda McKee eight hundred dollars as will show in my
entry book. To Joseph K.Porter one hundred acres of land
in Henry County, about two miles west of Paris. "I bequeath
to John A.Porter as part of his legacy and fifth of sale of
land in Carroll County 500 acres! To youngest son George
M.Porter to have one fifth of 500 acres of land in Carroll
County. Nominates three sons William, Thomas K, and James
D. Porter as executors. December 18, 1830. Signed William
Porter. Attest - Rees Thomas, and Robert D.Bowes. There is
a codicil to the will, in which he bequeathed to George W.
Wilcox and Sarah his wife certain property. Refers to
daughter Sarah D. wife of George W.Wilcox. Refers to his
son-in-law David W.Wilson and Eliza R.Wilson who was his
daughter. He had land on the waters of West Spring Creek in
Henry County, Tennessee which he left his son Joseph K.
Porter. The codicil was made 16th April 1832. It was signed
William Porter. Witnessed Robert D.Bouce (?) and Joseph
R.Porter. The second codicil follows in which he again
refers to his wife Agnes and to his son William. It is
signed and witnessed by the same parties.

Samuel Howard left will. dated 5 Feby 1833. He says
he is infirm with age. refers to "dear wife Mary" to have
household goods. Refers to "My sister Elizabeth". Wife
Mary and A.B. Witherington executors. (Wills 1832-34.p.12).

Will of Thomas Randle, deceased. dated 1832. To
Benjamin Peeples and wife, etc; To John Randle; To Richmond
Randle; To Thomas W.Randle. Signed by Samuel Hawkins, James
Leeper and Samuel McCorkle. This does not appear to be a will
but more names the heirs of Thomas Randle decd. (wills 1832-
34 p.25).

The court ordered to lay off years provisions for
Dorothy Ross late widow of Hammon Ross decd. 17 Dec. 1832.
(Wills 1832-34 p.51.).

Joseph Barton was guardian of Martha Ann, Joseph W.,
Margaret M., and Benjamin F.Barton,minor orphans of Benjamin
Barton, decd. 1832. (Wills 1832-34 p.54).

John Hardcastle was guardian for Jacob and Isaac Willoughby minor heirs and Andrew Willoughby was decd. March 2,
1833. (Wills 1832-34 p.55).

The court ordered settlement with James Leeper and
Elizabeth Stone executor and executrix of last will and testament of William Stone deceased. 1833. (Wills 1832-34 p.57).

The will of Alexander McCorkle Senir of Henry County,
Tennessee, calls for daughter Catherine, Daughter Nancy Andrews,
To son Alexander, To son Lewis, To son Samuel McCorkle. To
Joseph McCorkle. Grandson John Westley McCorkle. He refers to
the family Bible . He also refers to deceased son James H. Mc-
Corkle. Will probated 1833. (Wills 1832-34 p.65).

The will of Henry Stith deceased calls for Mrs. Mary M.
Stith widow of Brother Andrew all property that I purchased at
the sale of Andrew. Stith's estate now in her possession, etc.
To Andrew Stith two milch cows, etc. My two daughters Eliza
Caroline Northington and Elizabeth S.Stith both now in Virginia.
To Aricina Stith. Appoints my Brother Abner Stith executor.
30 June 1832. Signed Henry Stith. Proved Sept. Court 1833. (Wills
1832-34 p.100.).

The will of Alexander McCaud of Henry County, Tennessee.
Wife Margaret McCaul plantation and negroes, books, clock and H.H
goods. Children named , Son Milton, daughters Salley,Disy, Rachel,
Carlotte, Peggy, Son Joseph. Appoints son John McCaul executor
11 August 1833. Signed Alexander McCaul (Seal). Witnesses -
James Ray, Senr. Thomas Ray. (Wills 1832-34 p.104).

Isaiah Simmons left will dated Sept.22, 1833. Refers
to his growing crops to support the family. Wife Susan. She to
raise children. Wife and James N.Bass exec. Children not by
name. Signed Isaiah (X) Simmons. Witnesses. Edward Eblin,
William Palmer, John B. Fonville, and Phillip Halter (Hatter?)
(Wills 1832-34 p.122.)

The will of Ralph King deceased, provides To Anderson
Sturdivant my house etc. To Jesse Thomas $100.and schooling;
Refers to Andrew McCampbell. Mentions house and lot in town of
Paris. "My father David King of Warren County,North Carolina.
Appoints John J. Ervin (Erwin ?) and Doctor James Wilson as
executors. 12 December 1833. Witnessed by A.M.Hemtrannock and
John Barfield. (Wills 1832-34 p.126).

March 31, 1834 Lewis McCorkle guardian for Catherine
Ann McCorkle minor heir of James H.McCorkle. decd. (Wills 1832-
34 p.135).

March 24, 1834 John Hardcastle was guardian for
Jacob and Isaac Willoughby heirs of Andrew Willoughby, decd
(Wills 1832-34 p.137.).

James Haynes will, April 21, 1847. names Son Asa
Haynes, Daughter Ruth Haynes, Son Thomas Haynes, Son David
Haynes, Son Harry and son Jonathan Haynes. To the last
three named 214 acres of land. Grandson James son of Harry Haynes. Appoints David J. Kendall and Owen H.Edwards
executors. (Wills 1844-56 p.269).

John H. Diggs will. wife Sally place we now live
on 230 acres. Daughter Matilda. Daughter Mary. Son William
C., Diggs. Three youngest sons, Youngest James K.not 21
years of age. Son Harris. Five sons, Harris, William C.,
Robert, George and James K. all sons. To Mary Sophia
and Martha (not called children but indicated). Appoints
son Harris and wife Sally executors. 28 August 1848. (Wills
1844-56 p.273).

John B.House made his will 27 January 1846. Wife
Elizabeth tract of land I reside on. Children- Jane House,
Wm.L.House, Mildred Manda, John B.House. To wife for sup-
port of minor children. He owned many negroes. States that
he has given to his daughter Mary Jane House 2/3 of my stock
of hogs etc. To daughter Sarrah Ann Stovall property. To
daughter Martha House decd children Sarrah Elizabeth and
William Thomas House. To Elizabeth Ann Duke my daughter.
To daughter Mary Jane House. To son William I (j?) House,
To daughter Melvina F.House. To Daughter Manda C.House.
To Son John B.House. Divide between all children except
Martha Hays decd, her children. A-point William Duke and
Amos Milliken executors. (Wills 1844-56 p.276).

Thomas Bowden made his will which is on file in
Henry County. He refers to 'all my children" - Harriett
A. Oliver; Quentine J.Howard; Mathew T. Bowden; Caroline
B.Veasy; Catherine C. Carter; E.W. Bowden; Elizabeth B.
Millan; Margaret A. Rosser; Wilanth C.Bowden; Thos. W.
Bowden; Benj. J. Bowden; Sons Thos W. Bowden and Benj.T.
Bowden $100 each, complete their education. Appoints M.
L. Bowden, B.T.Bowden executors. Nov. 7, 1848. (Wills 1844-
1856 p. 278).

Zachariah Noel's will. Wife Polly. He owned considerable land. Refers to 50 acre tract. Mary Callaway a
granddaughter 'we" have raised $50.00. Appoints wife Polly
Noel and Elder James Morphis my executors. Second month of
1848. Signed Z Noel. (Wills 1844-1856 p.278).

Tabitha Bostick's will. To be buried in a decent
manner. To grandchildren born to me by the ties of nature
love and affection to wit - John D.Hart, Charles J.F. Hart,
Patience J.Lewis wife of Charles S. Lewis. James Wm.Hart

and Josephine P. Hart. Many slaves mentioned. My children
Jane Hart widow of John M.Hart decd. Grandchildren John J.
Hart, Charles J.Hart, Charles S.Lewis. January 26, 1846.
(Wills 1844-56 p.297.)

James Wilkerson made his will in this county , in
which he names his youngest son James K.Wilkerson. He refers to
Polly Ann Vaughn and her heirs. To grandson William E.Wilkerson.
Appoints H. Steely and James K. Wilkerson executors. 17 March
1849. (Wills 1844-56 p.315).

The will of Martin Neese, Senior, dated 16 March 1839,
calls for daughter Sarah Cotner land. Son John Neese decd ---
his heirs $1.00. Four sons and four daughters. William, Joseph,
Martin, Daniel and Elizabeth Neese. Sarah Cotner, Milly Cotter
and Nelly Robertson. Appoints Sons Martin and Daniel Neese executors. (wills 1844-56 p.326). Signed Martin (X) Neese.

William McGehee left a will in which he provided for
the support of his wife and family. Wife Ann to have land and
house. Educate children -- James Abraham McGehee and Mary
Louiza McGehee. Daughter Eliza Ann McGehee. Son John Walker
McGehee. Son James Abraham McGehee not 21 years of age. Daughter
Mary McGehee not 21 years of age. Appoints wife Ann and friend
John H. Dunlap executors. 24 April 1849. (Wills 1844-56 p.335)

Jeremiah Moody in his will stipulated that he wanted to
be buried in the Christian manner. Wife Elizabeth 1/3 of a
tract of land on which "I" live. Refers to the dwelling. refers
to "my children" Daughter Elijah Myrack 50 acres. Two sons James
Mathews Moody and Jeremiah Monroe Moody land. Son George W.
Moody and his children. Willis L. Williams certain property.
Appoints two sons William Moody and Samuel Moody executors. 18
October 1841. (Wills 1844-56 p.337).

The will of Susan Ann Williams shows that she left her
clothes to her mother. She states that she had an only brother
James Williams to whom she left the balance of the estate. She
appointed Ralph J.Williams executor. 7 January 1850. (Wills 1844-
56 p.346).

Watson Wimbush made his will February 11, 1850. To
daughters Martha, Rebecca, and Sarah he left property. To daughter Mary Ruby he left certain property. To his son Washington.
He mentions that he owned considerable land. He refers to his
heirs namely - John D., George R., Martha Hempt, Rebecca Jane,
Sarrah Ann , Washington Moody. Mary Rauten. Appoints brother
William R. Wimbush now being in Listuning County,Mississippi,
executor. Stipulates to educate "my" children. (Wills 1844-
56 p.346).

In his will Henry Smith names wife Susannah to have the
plantation. Son William to have 50 acres land. Son Samuel to have
50 acres of land. Youngest son Richard Smith. To Alfred G.Oliver

Sixteen dollars account. Four daughters Martha, Mary,Ann and Elizabeth Smith. Appoints Susannah Smith executrix. March 3, 1849 .(Wills 1844-56 p.356)

Milbry Atkins, widow of R.S. Atkins left a will, in which she names sons Green T.Atkins, George C.Atkins, Daniel L. Atkins, Joseph T.Atkins, Richard S. Atkins. The four youngest children - Milly Atkins, Baldwin Atkins, John Atkins, Rebecca L.Atkins. Appoints son G. T. Atkins, Geo.C. Atkins, D.L.Atkins, Joseph L. Atkins, and R.L. Atkins executors. April 3, 1850 (Wills 1844-56 page 369).

The will of Samuel C. Peay bears date Sept. 23, 1848. To his wife Mary G. he left a tract of land that they lived on. Names no children. Appoints friend P.J. Iron and Jesse C.Cooper as executors. (wills 1844-56 p. 385).

Elizabeth Cooper in her will provided to Thomas Crutchfield land in Henry County. Thomas Crutchfield's daughter E.B. Crutchfield the undivided half of land. He then names three sons of said Crutchfield, viz - Henry H., Hartall F., John B. Crutchfield. To" my nephew" J.C. Freeman, slaves. To Elizabeth B.Crutchfield slaves. Names Jeremiah Dumas and John C.Freeman as trustees for Elizabeth B.Crutchfield. Mentions Eliza Freeman to keep trunk and leave Elvira J.Freeman and John W. Cooper certain property. Sept. 17, 1850 (Wills 1844-56 p.391).

The will of Mary Muzzall is on the record and names son Jo.W. Muzzall. Son Wm.A Muzzall. Daughter Elizabeth Highlow. Granddaughter Mary Stewart. Grand-daughter Sarah Gooden (formerly Sarah Sorell). Grandson William D.Muzzall. Granddaughter Lyda Sorell. Appoints William A. Muzzall executor. 21 July 1849. (Wills 1844-56 p.399).

The will of William Crawford bears date 23 June 1851 To his wife he left the home where I now live 750 acres of land. Three sons, William L.Crawford, Samuel B. Crawford, and Joseph B.Crawford. He also names children - John S. Crawford, James M.Crawford, Louisa Looney and her daughter Sarah Jane Cloar, Elizabeth Hendrix and to the children of Mariah L.Frazier, Mary and Harold , and Catherine M. O. Hartsfield. To Wm.B.Crawford property. My three sons William L., J.B., and Joseph B. Crawford in bond pay to Mrs. Looney. (Wills 1844-56 p.402).

Albert G.Love made his will in which he names wife Mira Love all property I own except etc. etc. My children not all of age, not by name. Appoints his brother Samuel C. Love and wife Mira executors. May 29, 1851 (Wills 1844-56 p.40

        July 8, 1849 at Mount Stanhope, Sarah Heyland
Taylor made her will which is recorded in Henry County,
Tennessee. She refers to her sons Georgia Alexander and
John Thomas.   Daughters Hetty Ann 316 acres land equally
divided. My youngest daughter a minor , Sarah M.A.. The
third daughter Maria E., if she wishes to return to Ohio,and
live as one of the family , 100 acres land family privileges.
There is a mention of Dr. Lynch. There is an additional part
of the will which says "Since above written,death has depriv-
ed me of a dear and favored daughter, the delight of my life
and comfort of my heart. I am discharging to her children
parental care. My son William had a head right league of land."
To four heirs of the departed daughter Louisa E.H. Coleman
$1.00 to each. (Wills 1844-56 p. 404).

        The will of E.N. Cason, wife Sarah F. dated Oct. 9,
1845 is on record. (Wills 1844-56 p.20).

        Blount Cooper's will. Wife Elizabeth Cooper to have
negroes, furniture, Trunks, and land "I" live on for her life
or widowhood. Son Whitmell Cooper land he lives on."Sometime
about 1823-4 Joel Rogers and myself both of Wake County, North
Carolina" at time conveyed a certain negro boy named Charles
with others to Jubilee Rogers and John Rogers in trust for the
benefit and support of Whitmell Cooper and his wife Elizabeth
A. Cooper, and children. Whereas at court held at Dresden and
County of Weakley State of Tennessee, the said Jubilee Rogers
and John W.Rogers were released from the bother of said trust
and same given to Blount Cooper finding it not compitable
with interest of said Whitmell Cooper his wife Elizabeth and
children, etc. Mentions a tract of land in the center of
Henry County State of Tennessee about four miles from Paris
on the Huntington road 125 acres. B.Cooper settled said Whitmell his wife and children in some of the said land, etc. My
son-in-law William A.Tharp to have negroes. Daughter Mary
Cooney her life to have negroes, and at her death to her
son James F.Cooney who is not yet 21 years of age. Mary
Cooney's husband was James Cooney (in another place he is
called John Cooney). My children, sons Edward B.Cooper, Jesse
C.Cooper, John W.Cooper, Son-in-law Hanabell Harris and his two
sons Coathand C.Harris and Howell B.Harris. My granddaughter
Jane E.Harris, My granddaughter Jane Ellenor Harris (her
brothers say Coathand C and Howell B.). My granddaughter Jane
E.Harris. Son Whitmell Cooper, his children, namely- Wm.Cooper,
John Cooper, Jessie Cooper, Whitmell Cooper, Jeraleen Cooper,
Elizie Cooper. My daughter Sally A. Tharp (Thorp?). My daughter Jane Harris and her children,namely- Coathand C.Harris, Howell B.Harris, and Jane Ellenor Harris. Daughter Mary Cooney and
her husband John Cooney. Land in Hickman County,Kentucky named
the "Chalk Bank" upon the Mississippi River, 640 acres sold F.
Cayce in the year 1839. Son-in-law William A. Tharp (Thorp).
Executors sons Edward B., Jesse C., and John W.Cooper. Jany 1,
1845. Signed B. Cooper. (Wills 1844-56 p.21).

John Brooks will. Names wife Mary to whom he
leaves the plantation. Daughter Acona Crittendon. Daughter Sarah Hutcherson. Son Thomas. Mentions William H.
Brooks, Harry Brooks, James W.Brooks, Lucy Samma Brooks.
Pleasant Hampton Brooks. The children of my dead son
Jessie Brooks, equal share belonging to my son Jesse if he
were living. To Clinton Brooks, Dillard Brooks, Ann Brooks,
and Mary Brooks,children of my deceased son William Brooks,
their father's share. To son John Brooks equal share.
To sons Culpepper Brooks and Thomas Brooks land I live on
equally divided, pay their sister Betsey Phillips $300. My
daughter Elizabeth Phillips. Son Michael Brooks $100. equal
share. My wife Mary. Appoints son Michael and son Thomas
Brooks as executors 12 July 1843. (Wills 1844-56 p.25).

The will of Armstead W.Forest. 10 Nov. 1845 named
Elizabeth as his wife and to her bequeathes 195 acres of
land, Barren fork of West Sandy in Henry County.Collectable
money coming to us in the State of Virginia from the estate
of Robert Forest decd also from estate of John Forest who
died intestate of Halifax County,Virginia. My boy Coleman
is a dwarf. My friend John Bushart at my death to take
charge of my wife and property to manage, etc. Friend A.W.
Bachus to have Jackson & Colt and to be interested at his
death by his son John Newton Bacus. At my wife's death
my friend John Bushart to have all the tract of land. At
his death to his son Jackson Newton Bushart. At my wife's
death Miss Mary Ann Bushart to have slaves and Mary Frances
Bachus to have a slave. To friend John Bushart my iron
gray colt. Give a colt to friend Adolphus W. Bachus.
(Wills 1844-56 p.27).

John W.Cooper of McCracken County, Kentucky, but
having effects in Henry County, Tenn, did die intestate and
Walter H.Caldwell became administrator . January 1846. Wills
1844-56 p.35).

John Atkins left will in which he devised to his
daughter Martha M. Ivis the wife of Dennis G.Ives (could be
Jones ??) 237½ acres in Henry County, Tenn. Daughter Evaline
Harris wife of Wm.B.Harris 260 acres land. Son Eldridge
G.Atkins 740 acres and etc. Son John Dewit Clinton Atkins
and son William L.T.Atkins. Two youngest sons William
Edward Travis Atkins and James Knox Polk Atkins. Wife
Mary S.Atkins. Owned much land. Appointed son-in-law Wil-
liam B.Harris and son Eldridge G.Atkins and wife Mary S.
Atkins executors. 27 Sept. 1844.(Wills 1844-56 p.35).

The will of John Yow dated 26 October 1838, names
his wife Elizabeth. He had books bonds and notes. Daughter
Therry Robinson; daughter Elizabeth Henry Bushart; Daughter
Gray Jagster;daughter Syntha Adaleen; Daughter Eliza Ann;
Two sons John B and Wyatt C.Yow. (Wills 1844-56 p.40).

29 December 1845, John Ellis made his will. Mentions daughter Martha Ellis and Lucretia Ellis. Wife Krugah Ellis for her life certain property. Son Joseph Ellis. Daughter Rebecca Madlock wife of Samuel Madlock, Elizabeth Gunn, wife of George W.Gunn, Edna Dunham wife of Washington Dunham. Mallery Sexton wife of James Sexton. Margarett Fitch wife of Anderson Fitch. Martha and Lucreatis Ellis. Appoints James Ellis and Joseph Ellis executors. 29 Dec. 1845.(Wills 1844-56 p.79).

The will of Jacob Marberry names two daughters Mary Jane and Elizabeth Marberry. Two sons Abraham and Jacob N. Marberry, not of age. Refers to the farm. Youngest son not 21 years of age. The farm to support the family. Son Pleasant H. Marberry $600 advanced. Son Francis W.Marberry $550 advanced. Daughter Bashela Williams wife of Wm.Williams, the value of $425. Owned many negroes. Son Abraham 50 acres of land, "Emory Tract" and 100 off east end I live on. 8 Jany. 1846. (Wills 1844-56 p.125).

Hamblin F.Manly will. Wife Fanny have provisions. Granddaughter Harriett L.Hudson wife of Richard Hudson, decd. Son Richard Manley and my seven grandchildren to wit, Harriett F.Hudson wife of Richard Hudson, deceased. Geraldine Manley wife of Wm. C. Manley, Emmerly Manley wife of Isaac N.Manley, Ashley N.Randle, Susan Randle, Martha Randle, and George W. Randle. Son Richard Manley to have negroes, 640 acres land I live on less my said wife's dower which lies South and west of Reynoldsbury adjoining John Easters tract. To granddaughter Geraldine Manley wife of William C.Manley negroes. To my daughter (granddaughter) Evaline Manley wife of Isaac N.Manley, to have negroes. To granddaughter Susan F.Randle, daughter of John H.Randle and Delphy Randle. To Martha W. Randle sister of Susan F, etc. Grandson Ashley N.Randle 150 acres adjoining Geo. W.S. Randle. Grandson George W.L. Randle 150 acres land. Appoints son Richard Manly executor. 14 March 1846.There was an addition to the will added 14 March 1846. (Wills 1844-56 p.128).

The will of William Ellison dated October 17, 1843, provides for support and education of children. Wife Vincey. Son James 10 acres land I live on. Wife executrix. (Wills 1844-56 p.135).

Edward Travis, left will in which he refers to negroes to remain in possession of John G. Harris, the Executor named ,until after the youngest child arrives at age of 18 years, then to be liberated (certain negroes). Daughter Martha M.Harris wife of Isham G.Harris certain slaves. Son Edward L.Travis negroes. Daughter Elizabeth C.Glesson wife of Glesson certain slaves. Two Robert L. Travis his heirs and etc. Son Jesse H.Travis. Son Benjamin W.Travis. Daughter Sarah M. Warren wife of D.Westly Warren. Son Wm.G. Travis. Son James L.Travis. son Ludson W.Travis and grandson John Westly Crutchfield $200 when 21 years of age. Grandchildren James and Thomas McMeans. My children, Elizabeth C.,

Robert L., Joseph H., Benjamin W., Sarah M., Martha M.,
Wm.G., James L., and Ludson W. leaving out my oldest
son Edward L. and the representatives of my daughter
Margarett McMeans. Appoints Isham H. Harris of Paris,
Tenn. executor. And appoints his guardian to Ludson W.
Travis. Sept. 10, 1846. (Wills 1844-56 p.135). Note-
Isham Greene Harris was born at Tullahoma, Tennessee on
February 10, 1818. He moved to Paris in 1838, studied
law and began practice in 1841. He was a member of the
Legislature in 1847, a candidate for presidential elector
in 1848 and a member of Congress from 1849 to 1853. He
opened a law office in Memphis in 1853 and was chosen presidential elector 1856. He was elected Governor of Tennessee in 1857, 1859 and 1861. After the election of President Abraham Lincoln he became a strong advocate of sec-
ession and in 1861 issued the proclamation declaring Tennessee out of the American Union. At the close of the war he
went to Mexico, but returned to Memphis in 1867. In 1876
he was elected United States Senator and continued .in
office until his death in Washington D.C., July 1897.

The will of Alexander H.Kane, dated Sept. 2, 1846
provides for his sister Mary June Wilson wife of William
Wilson of the State of Mississippi, land on Wadesborough
Road, now occupied by I.Worthan, and to be divided between
eldest daughter and youngest son of my said sister. To
Charlotte G.Youton of Missouri $500. To sister Lucinda
Ready of the State of Illinois $75.00. To Elizabeth and
Lucinda Kane daughters of my late brother Edward Kane, decd
$1000. To sister in law Hannah Kane of County of Armagh in
Ireland widow of my late brother John Kane, decd, certain
property. Refers to Co-partnership between "myself" and
James Wortham of firm of Kane & Worthan to continue. My
brother David Kane of Armagh aforesaid. My sister Elizabeth
Nephew John Kane now residing with me $1500. Brother-in-
law Wm.Wilson. Appoints Benjamin C.Brown and James C.Car-
rier of Henry County, executors. Nephew John Kane not yet
21 years of age. (Wills 1844-56 p.138).

James Kendall left will in which he mentions his
daughter Martha Lee a tract of land whereon she and her
husband now live 63½ acres; Son John Kendall; Son William
Kendall: Son Alvin Kendall: Son Thomas Kendall; Son Willson
Kendall: Daughter Mary Kendall; Son James Kendall; daughter
Sarah Kendall; daughter Martha Lee; Wife Sarah 1000 lbs.
Dated Sept. 12, 1846. (Wills 1844-56 p.144).

Richard Wright left will in which he names daughter
Mary Stubblefield to her certain negroes and plantation.
Son William Stubblefield. Appoints son William executor.
9 August 1841. (Wills 1844-56 p.146).

The will of John Crittendon recites that he is
weak of body. Son Aby A.Critendon. Son June Critendon.
Shelby T.Critendon, Ellen L.Critendon, James K.P.Critendon

when of age. Wife Naomi property for life. "my children"
William Critendon, Charley Critendon, Mary Sullivant,
Elizabeth Wagster, Lewis A. Lewis Blake. Aby A. Critendon.
June Critendon, Jane Catherine Critendon, Shellby L. Crit-
endon, Ellen L. Crittendon. James K.Polk Crittendon. 29
October 1846. (Wills 1844-56 p.149).

    The will of Harris Berry dated 2 October 1846 names
his wife Meeky Berry to have land "I" live on 220 acres. My
children William Alfred Augustine Lafayette and Piety Geans.
Grandson William H.Oliver (or Olive ?) $200 when 21 years of
age. Grandson William H.Oliver division to go to the other
children. Desire Lafayette Berry and Augustine Berry to be made
equal to Wm.Alfred and Piety Geans. Appoints Wm.and Augustine
executors.   (Wills 1844-56 p. 160.)

    William Thurston left will. Wife Mary land "I" bought of
G.Gore upon which I now live. Land adjoining John Crittendon and
Driver's line. The road intersectd road leading from Pleasant
View to mouth of Sandy etc. Passes B.T. Bowden and Chas. Brooks.
Son-in-law William Thurston have land. Granddaughter Rebecca
Davis. Wm.Davis, Zarrah Davis, Eveline Davis, Henrietta Thurston
daughter of Wm.Thurston. All children not yet of age. Appoints
Wm.Thurston and Benjamin T. Bowden as executors. 12 January
1847 (Wills 1844-56 p.163).

    The will of James W.Taylor,named wife Edith Taylor.
Three sons James S., Joseph W., and Isaac W. Taylor. He had a
farm. He mentions the burying ground. To my son James "I" give my
Declaration of Independence, surrounded with coat of arms of
each State in a Mahogany frame also Mitchells large reference and
distance map. etc. Son Joseph a large likeness of my brother
Joseph Taylor deceased, together with the dress wood which my
father aforesaid carried through the last war also my atlas map.
To my son Isaac my son and his mother's likeness. My sister $100
Books in the library to my sons Joseph and Isaac. One Medical book
to son James. My papers, letters etc, all kinds to three sons on
decease of wife. Appoints wife Edith S.Taylor and sons James
Taylor and Matthew C.Bowles as executors. 1845. Codicil. His son
James was a Doctor of Physics. (Wills 1844-56, p.183).

    John Pritchett made will in which names wife Susannah to
have negroes. One half net estate of Joe Fresher, deceased of
the State of Virginia which is now in suit James Pritchett of the
State of Virginia Admr. Wife land I live on. Land od Old Dresden
Road. Son James Pritchett of Virginia one half not proceeds of
money record of estate of James Fisher deceased of which James
Pritchett is administrator. Daughter Aurella Pritchett $1000 .
Son Geo.P.Pritchett. Divide land six parts. son James of Virginia.
Son A.C.Pritchett. Son George P.Pritchett. One childs part to heirs
of W.C. Pritchett, deceased. One sixth part to granddaughter Jane
Aurella Dugger. Appoints sons James and A.C. Pritchett as executors.
12 Feb.1846. Codicil 24 Feb 1847. (name Fresher could be Fisher.).
(Wills 1844-56 p.211.).

Joseph Alexander left will. Names wife Flora. Daughter Margarett and rest of children not by name. To receive part of estate of Asa Atkins. Appoints Josiah Owens and Erasom Ham executors. 19 July 1847 .(Wills 1844-1856 p.214).

The 21st of June 1847 Lucy Williams made her will and names oldest daughter Rebeca Wills $10.00. Son Ralph Williams to have a mare. Rest divided between my children. One LARGE BIBLE I give to my grandson Garbee J. Williams. Appoints Youngdest son Ralph J.Williams as executor. (Wills 1844-56 p. 215.).

Mary P.Randle left a will which devised to her sister Amy Emerson's children $1.00 each. To her sister Lucy Travis's children $1.00 each. Sister Elizabeth Jernigan $1.00. Niece Mary Elizabeth Walters, daughter of my sister Tab.G.Walters. Land in Henry County, Tenn. Aunt Susan Randle keep and raise my niece until of age. My niece Mary Elizabeth Walters my gold watch. Appoints Aunt Susan Randle and J.A. Chambers executors. August 24, 1847 (Wills 1844-56 p.215).

Susan Ball's will. Widow and relict of the late John Ball of Halifax County, Virginia. Son James Ball of the County of Vago and State of Indiana, in trust for use of my daughter E.H. Arost, formerly Elizabeth Ball, land in Vargo Indiana. To son William J.Ball of County and State aforesaid for use of John Ball, Joseph P. Ball, and Charles Ball minor heirs of my beloved son Joseph P.Ball, deceased land in Clay County,Indiana. Son William James Ball tract of land in Clay County,Indiana. I give and bequeath nothing to children of my first husband Joseph Parker deceased because they have been fully and amply provided for. Appoints son Wm.James Ball executor. 17 July 1846. (Wills 1844-56 p.221.).

Joseph Barton will. Wife Sophia W.Barton. My boy John D.W.Barton 150 acres I live on. And Mansion house and land. Appoints Dempsey Bowden guardian for son D.W. Barton, not yet of age. Some property to be divided amongst my children and grandchildren except daughter Martha Mcrab (?) widow of John Mcrab (?) deceased, having already given her. To children of John Gore of Illinois portion of my estate. He married my Sophis now dead. That portion of my estate that their mother would have had and appoints said John Gore guardian to their children. The four children of my son Benjamin Barton deceased. Appoints James Walker and Moses Todd executors. 4 July 1843.(Wills 1844-56 p.230).

The will of James Gleason, 1847. Son Dermis Gleason 50 acres of land. Son Daniel Gleason. Son James Gleason. Rest of my children mentioned not by name. Daughters Martha Mc ? Daughter Elizabeth Norman; Heirs of Nancy Flake.Appoints

R.L. Thomason executor. (Wills 1844-56 p.235.)

Aruella Pritchett's will. Niece Jane Aurella Dugger.
My brother A.C.Pritchett. J.A.Dugger. My father willed me
money. A.C.Pritchett's heirs. My brother Wm.C. Pritchett.
Step-mother Susannah Pritchett. Brother James Pritchett executor. 24 Dec. 1847 . (Wills 1844-56 p.235).

The will of Samuel Arnett refers to his wife but does
not call her name. Son Andrew J. Arnett. Appoints George W.
Arnett, executor. May 12, 1844. (Wills 1844-56 p.236).

John Williams , Jr's will. Son Benjamin Wilkerson
Williams. The eldest to be executor. For youngest son .The
eldest son to look after property for youngest son. Youngest son
Elisha Williams 100 acres land. To Delilah Hand 100 acres land.
Youngest daughter Martha Williams. 19 May 1846 (Will 1844-56 p,
237.)

The will of William P.Duke. Son William land on Bird's
Creek 312 acres being same whereon "I" now reside. Daughter
Nancy C.Cook $1.00. Grandson William P. Yarborough $1.00
Granddaughter Elizabeth M.Yarborough $1.00. Son William to be
executor. 6 Jan. 1843 (Will 1844-56 p.239).

Will of Darling Jones."I, Darling Jones of the County
of Henry and State of Tennessee, calling to mind the uncertainty
of life and the certainty of death and being of sound mind, at
this time, I do hereby publish and declare this to be my last will
and testament, revoking and making void all other wills by me at
any time made. etc. Wife Margaret Jones. My granddaughter not of
age. Grandson McHuston Stephenson. Three granddaughters Susan
Cole, Betsy Ann Tyler, Katherine McConnell, share equally. My
granddaughter Katherine McConnell. Daughter Louisa Jones to have
$100. Appoints Robert McConnell executor. 24 April 1850.(Wills
1844-56 p.430.).

Jacob Bushart Senior will. Two sons John and ___ ?
Bushart. Beloved Nancy Bushart my wife. Children, Elizabeth
Richardson, John Buchart,Nancy Bushart, Jacob Bushart, Sally
Bushart, Ann Suter, Caleb Bushart, Daniel Bushart, and Polly
Caldwell. Two sons John and Harry executors. March 23, 1848. (Will
1844-56 p.431).

Celia Darnell will. To May Jane Aycock (formerly Mary
Jane Upchurch) to have negro girl. To Celia Elizabeth Wynns (formerly C.E. Upchurch) to have negro. To Bayliss House Upchurch to
have negro. To John F. (not 21 years of age) and Georgw W.
Upchurch to have negroes. To Eli Upchurch a negro girl. To
Jennetta Darnell for life certain property. Appoints Thomas J.Wynns
and Jordan T. Aycock executors. 10 May 1848. (Wills 1844-56,
p. 433).

Will of Margery Hooper, Three children Mary Ann Hooper,

Margery Edmons Payler (could be Taylor ?) and John Sackland Hooper, $2.00 each. John Sackland Hooper, son, 1/3
of all. Appoints son John Sackland Hooper executor. 16 Oct.
1838. (Wills. 1844-56 p.434).

Susan S.Randle's will. May 6, 1852. Money in hands
of Elbert L. Randle loan to him. My son Edwin H. Randle. My
grandson Eldridge R.Hall $2000. My grandchildren not by name.
Son Edwin H. Executor. (Wills 1844-56 p.444).

The will of William Crawley, Senior. 14 June 1852
---Daughter Mary Ann Walton $20.00. Son Jackson's heirs to
have $100.00 (divide between four children not of age).Son
Wm.Crawley take charge of land. Wife Rebecca household
goods and money. Son William Crawley charge of his mother
so long as she lives. (Wills 1844-56 p.446).

Walker Taliaferro made his will 8 May 1852. Refers
to wife for her life not by name however. At her death to
children not by name. Appoints Chas. S.Yancey and E.T.
Taliaferro executors. (Wills 1844-56 p.446).

The will of Mary Copeland bears date 23 April
1852 ---In it she states her daughter Louisa to have certain
property and that the said daughter is the now wife of Daniel
Mathis. She refers to "My other children" but does not call
them by name. Names John Haynes as executor. (Wills 1844-
56 p.454).

Peter Owen made his will 5 July 1852. He refers to
ALL his children but does not call them by name. The name of
his wife was Elizabeth and he appoints as executor Anderson A
Clark. (Wills 1844-56 p.455).

The next will I have to give you is a little con-
fusing. It seems to be that of Susan Hodge, but it goes on to
read " Divide property between wife and children" which makes
it found like a gentleman's will and not a woman's will. She
further names as her executors W.H.Carter and R.F.Carter. It
is dated 30 August 1852. (Wills 1844-56 p.455).

The will of James Lawson , 17 March 1846 , names his
wife Juritha to have property for life. Daughter Jane John-
ston Lawson, only living child. Wife and daughter to be the
executrix. (wills 1844-56 p.468).

James Hicks Senior left will. -- wife Susannah A.
Hicks. Daughter Susan W.Hicks. "My brother Wm.Hicks"."My
six children" Rushad W., Gideon E.Harrison, Susan W., James,
and Francis M.Hicks. Daughter Nancy W.Holland and my sin-in-
law Sparman Holland. Son John B.Hicks. Daughter Amanda A.
Travis and son-in-law Robert L.Travis. Appoints sons Gideon
E. and Harrison Hicks executors. 8 April 1852. (Wills '44-'56.p

William Lefever's will. 29 October 1852. To Mary
Fowler $5.00. To John Lefever, Sarah Isabella and Harriett,
Josephine and Narcissa these $5.00. To John Lefever land.
All my children not yet of age. Wants equal division to all
except Mary Fowler. Appoints Wm.Coleman executor. (Wills
'44-'56 p. 473).

Amanda M.F.Palmer's will. 6 June 1853. She provides
that " my own mother and sister Virginia be enclosed with
palings and a paid of stones put up, out of my estate." Sister
Sarah Smith Palmer to have certain negroes. Brother Edward H.
Sister Tennessee Thomas to have money. Sister Tennessee and
sister Sarah Smith and brother Edward. Appoints Edmond M.
Palmer as executor. (Wills 1844-56 p.536.)

The will of John Grainger bears date 18 December
1851. Wife Nancy land. To Henry Grainger $10.00 for school-
ing. Geo W.Grainger, equal with other children. Mary Grainger
my youngest daughter. Wife Nancy and Josiah Porter to be
executrix and executor. (wills 1844-56 p.540).

John Field's will names wife Martha. Two daughters
Martha and Freelove to live with their mother also Mary Kennedy and her little children while they remain single. Property
to be equally divided at my wife's death except Bennett Fields
and Nancy Beeman they already have received. Mentions Edmond
Beeman. "My heirs" Ruby Martha Levison, Freelove and Nancy Ann
Frances the heirs of Nancy Beeman. (no comma between the
names). Appoints John and Seth Fields executors. 17 Sept. 1844.
Wills 1844-56 p.547).

The will of Susannah Pritchett names niece Mary M.
Pritchett for her life. To niece M.P. my entire interest in my
brother James Fisher's estate that which I shall mention in my
will. At niece death divide between her and A.C. Pritchett's
children. Appoints A.C. Pritchett trustee to manage property.
The children of A.C. Pritchett and his wife Nell Pritchett to
have certain items. My niece Adaline Wilson. All of Jackson
and Wilson children except James F.Jackson. To Mary Doty of
Virginia ($500 due me in my brother James Fisher's estate). My
sister Ann E.Marberry. To Susan F.Green. Appoints Armstead C.
Pritchett executor , 1 June 1849. Codicil--$500 before willed
sister Marberry,"My sister being dead revoke and make void that
section of the will pertaining to her. To Benjamin Sterling
Pritchett son of A.C. $500. Benj.Sterling Pritchett not of age.
The date of the will not shown.Probably probated in 1853.(Wills
1844-56 p.548.).

Henderson Baucum's will. 16 Dec. 1853. Wife Mary M.L.
Children -- David Clark George Ransom William Henderson, Sarah
Elizabeth and Martha Mary Lee Baucum. (cannot tell if all one
name of several) Appoints John L.Smith Exec. (Wills 1844-56 p.558).

John M.Williams left will in which he names wife Nancy to have 200 acres of land. He also names grandson John M.L. Williams. To daughter Elizabeth Owens 200 acres of land. Grandson Benj.W.Williams to have 50 acres of land. Son-in-law Evan Wallace and heirs to have 90 acres in Stewart County, Tennessee. Granddaughter Nancy Wallace to have 50 acres on Eagle Creek. Elisha Williams " my son" $5.00. Heirs of son John who is deceased. 29 October 1853. (wills 1844-56 p.587).

June 5, 1854 J.B.Cooper executed his will at the house of Frances Emily Cooper and Elizabeth Cooper . He names Nancy Ann Cooper and Willis H. Cooper , also Joseph John Cooper . They are to keep the house six years then it is to be sold and divided between my children. He does not call these his children but it is inferred. James Cooper made executor. (wills 1844-56 p.588).

William Hill wrote his will 28 January 1850 in which he named his wife Mary to have certain property for her life. Son Jeremiah Hill. Children-- William E.Hill, Penelope K.Hill, Jeremiah Hill, All of the children are not of age. Daughters Sarah VanCleave, Elizabeth Nance , Nancy Holden, Frances Guinn, Mary A.Nance, Isabel C. Potts. Martha Pierce. Son Spencer Hll to have 100 acres of land -- Son Joseph W Hill to have 100 acres of land - - son John N. Hill to have 100 acres of land. (wills 1844-56 p.588).

The will of Sarah Worsham provides for John W.W. Crutchfield (the son of John Crutchfield and Mary his wife) to have slaves. The rest of the property to be divided be- tween Sarah M. Warren (wife of Dr. W.Warren).Martha M.Harris (wife of Isham G.Harris), Wm.E.C.Travis , and James L.Travis, Ludson W.Travis and John W.W. Crutchfield. Sept. 23, 1852. (wills 1844-56 p.604.)

Willie Williford left will, 23 April 1852. Names son Willis Willie Williford land he is now on. Names his wife as Elizabeth who is to have the rest of the land. He refers to a daughter but does not call her by name. Appoints his son as executor. (wills 1844-56 p.605).

March 11, 1850 is the date that Elisha Peel made his will in which he named his wife Ann Peel. He also names a step-daughter Nancy E.Joiner. A son John Peel. A son Bryant Peel. Appoints wife Ann and son Bryant executors. (Wills 1844-56 p.619).

The will of John Upchurch dated 30 April 1853, names son Jesse. Four sons John, Bayless, George and Eli are mentioned, also son Joshua who was deceased at that time. Then he names three sons William, Jesse and Thomas L. of my daughter Catherine Darnell all land South of Beaver Dam Creek except 20 acres. Granddaughter Sarah Jane Yancey. Son David

Upchurch. Heirs of my son James Jackson Upchurch to have land. Sons Jesse and David executors. (wills 1844-56 p.621).

G.W.Orr made his will on 27 May 1853, He names children James Jesse Bedford Syrus Elisha Rebecca Ann (no commas between) divide equally. All children not of age. Wife Nancy. Brother S. G. Orr and E.D. Paschall executors. 27 May , 1852 .(Wills 1344-56 p.638).

James Tart in his will dated 14 March 1855 calls for his wife Juliet. Three children are named, viz - Penbroke Summersette and Thadden Constantine Sovisky and Martha Virginia. (wills 1844-56 p.653).

The will of John C.Thompson, August 23, 1853, names wife Middly M. Nathaniel Porter as executor. There is a reference to a guardian for wife Middy M. (wills 1844-56 p.654).

Howel Edmonds will is dated 15 December 1853. He devised to Martha Hern who is now living with me $2000. She live on the plantation. Divide between her three children Susan Ann,Harvel Nicholas and John Crawford Hern. The children shall have their names altered from Susan Ann Hern to Susan Ann Edmonds, from Howel Nicholson Hern to Edmonds. From John Crawford Hern to Edmonds by the State of Tenn. The children not of age 21 years as yet. The children are to be cared for. Appoints Benj.C. Brown executor. (wills 1844-56 p.655).

The will of Lucretia Tennessee Biles names brother Thomas L. Biles to have certain negroes. Her sister to have property. Her sist's name Catherine Dillahunty. Two nieces Nancy Tennessee and Minerva Catherine Hays. Niece Harriet Biles. Niece Nancy Helen Dillahunty. Names her brother Thomas L.Biles as executor. December 19, 1854.(Wills 1844-56 p.656).

Gideon Davis, left will dated 9 March 1855. Names daughter Louisa William Dobby wife of John Dobby. Son Alexander Davis. Daughter Ann Mildred Peel wife of Lawrence E.Peel. Daughter Virginia Caroline to have tract of land 101 acres. Appoints Charles S. Lewis executor. (wills 1844-56 p.657).

The will of Emery Dent Prior is recorded on page 703 of Will Book 1844-56 in Henry County. Tennessee, but was probated in Johnson County, Illinois.

The wills of James Johnson, Samuel Anderson, Thomas B. Darby, Albert G. Cherry, T.P. Jernigan, James Conyers, John Wall, William Nance, James Walker, William C.Rogers, William Henry, and Dabney D.Byrd, are all recorded between 1854 and 1856 in Henry County, Tenn.

Isaac Searcy was made administrator of the Estate of Francis Richardson, decd. (Henry Co.Min Book. 1825-28.p.4).

Peter Kendall was named administrator of the Estate of Cynthia Kendall decd. Dec. 12, 1825 (Court Min. book 1825-28.p.5).

William V.Matthews late of the City of Louisville, Kentucky,now temporarily stopping near Point Clear in Baldwin County, Alabama, makes will. Wife Annie L. Mathews, Son Robert Linn (?) Matthews. (or Lewis). Father Robert Mathews, of Paris, Tenn. Mr. Charles Leus (?) of Montgomery, Alabama, July 1872. Dated Oct.20, 1871. Filed in Baldwin County, Alabama. Recorded also in Henry County, Tenn. (Will 1863-1878.p.507).

John M. Comer's will. names Three Daughters Martha, Lucy R., and Emily G.children who have died before their mother. Daughter Lucy . Nov. 27, 1860. (Wills 1864-78 p. 505).

Wiley J.Comer will of Henry County, Tennessee. Wife Emily Ann Comer. Youngest daughter Mattie Gillespie Comer. Two oldest daughters. Son Edward A.Comer $50.00. Daughter Sarah Frances wife of I.S. Roseberry. Daughter Eliza Jane wife of S.R. Shaw. Daughter Harriett Ann wife of A.J.Shaw. Daughter Susan wife of J.A. Campbell. Son Wm. Greaf Comer, who left me before 21 years of age, has not received any-thing. Son Edward A.Comer. Appointed oldest son Edward A. Comer executor. Aug. 31, 1869. (Wills 1364-78 p.521.).

Thomas Humphrey will. Wife Sally all of the land etc. Daughter Ila. Daughter Ann McLain. children namely, Jane Jones, Wm.D.Humphreys, James E.Humphreys, Henly Humphrey, and Abner Humphrey. Eldest daughter Ann McLain. Appoints Will D.Humphrey, James P/Humphrey executors. Nov. 6, 1859. Probated. (Wills 1856-63 p.374)

Invoice of sale of John Olive decd sold by Samuel Olive and A. Phillips admrs. on same.11 Oct.1859. (Wills 1856-63 p.446).

Invoice of sale of Josey Olive, decd, sold Nov.17, 1859. (Wills 1856-63 p.451.).

Mrs. Sarah A.Dunlap's will. To my sister Mrs. Ellen J Ozburn diamond ring. To my sister Ellen J.Ozburn. If she die to Mrs. Sue G.Dawson. Niece Hallie Dawson. Nieces Darling and Hallie Dawson. Appoints S.A. Champion executor. Aug. 25, 1882. Signed Sarah A. Dunlap. Witnessed Sue G.Dawson. Ellen J.Ozburn. Proved Nov. 1882 (Wills 1879-1902 p.39).

Mrs. Marietta Dunlap will. January 28, 1893. Two sons Richard W. and Wm.A. Dunlap. Money in hands of Charles G. Porter in Nashville. Proved Nov. 22, 1894. (Wills 1879-1902 p.252).

INDEX TO WILLS 1856-1663

* * * *

None listed in index in letter A. (Wills only listed here).

INDEX TO WILL BOOK 1822-1827

* * * * *

NOTE: This book contains all sorts of records,
wills are few but scattered. ERW

===

Dots and Dashes

Harvey E. Aden was born in Charleston, South Carolina, in 1808. When young moved to Simpson County,Kentucky and from there to Williamson County, Tennessee where he married in 1829 Louisa M.Brown. He was a carpenter. He died October 27, 1884. Louisa M.Brown was born in Lunenburg County, Virginia in 1811 and moved to Williamson County,Tennessee young. This couple were the parents of Judge Clinton Aden born at Paris, Henry County, Tennessee, October 12, 1835. He attended Bethany College in Virginia under Alexander Campbell for two years. After working as a carpenter twenty three years began the study of law under Judge McCampbell and later attended Cumberland University and was licensed by Judge Fitzgerald and Judge Williams in 1859. He practiced his profession until 1861; enlisted in the Confederate Army in Capt. Conway's Company of the 5th Regiment and was promoted to Captain in a cavalry company of the 10th Tennessee. He was in service until the close of the war. He then resumed the practice of law and was appointed Judge of the 1th Circuit. In 1865 he married Mary Fuqua of Carroll County, Tennessee. They had seven children, John B., Harvey F., William H., Clinton, Shelia, Thomas B., and Mary L. Aden.

John L. Lemonds was born October 6, 1837 in Henry County near the Kentucky line, the son of Robert and Eleanor H.(Martin) Lemonds, natives of North Carolina, but reared in Henry County. The father was a Blacksmith. Eleanor H.Lemonds died Dec. 9,1869.

J.R.B.Dinwiddie was born in Henry County, Feb. 2, 1828 the son of James and Mary (Carson) Dinwiddie , natives of Virginia. James Dinwiddie died in Henry County in 1860. On February 22, 1860 J.R.B..Dindiddie married Sallie Lee Gordon. To their union were born nine children.

John M. Coffman married Elizabeth White who was born near Louisville, Kentucky about 1797. John M. Coffman was born in Davidson County, Tennessee in 1799, the son of Isaac Coffman born in North Carolina, an early settler of Davidson County, Tennessee. John M. and Wlizabeth (White) Coffman had a son Wm.M.Coffman born in Henry County, Tennessee in 1833. John M. Coffman served in the War of 1812.

William L.Carter Jr. was an attorney at Paris, Henry County, Tennessee. He was born in the county in 1848, the son of W.L. and Mary (Biles) Carter. She died 1829. William L. Carter was born in Davidson County, Tennessee in 1803 and died in Henry County, Tennessee in 1824. William L. Carter married as his second wife Arabella Sessum of Humphrey Co. who died May 1886.

ESTATES, GUARDIANS, ORDERS, ETC.

* * * * * *

Polly Sikes was the widow of Samson Sikes, decd, Court of Dec. 12, 1825 (Court Min. 1825-1828 p.11).

Delilah Piper widow of Samuel Piper, decd, Dec. 12, 1825. (Court Min. 1825-28 p.11).

The court of December 13, 1825 refers to the trustees of the Paris Academy. (Min.Book 1825-28 p.14.)

Court Order regards Jesse C.Faunehill, regards to Elizabeth Richardson and Henry Richardson,minor orphans of Francis Richardson. Dec. 13, 1825 (Min.Book 1825-28 p.18)

A suit entered Wednesday Dec. 14, 1825-- James M. Wade Admr. VS. The heirs of Seth Wade, decd.(Court Min.1825-1828 p. 22).

The court granted permission for the Masonic Society to use a room upstairs in the Courthouse for meeting. Dec. 13, 1825 .(Court Min. 1825-28 p.25).

December 16, 1825 a deed was proved from Henderson Lewis to James R.Russell for one undivided seventh part of 253 acres of land in Albemarle County,Virginia.(Ct.Min. 1825-28 p.33).

The Court of December 16,1825 (Min.Book 1825-28 p. 34) William C.Rodgers and others VS. Reuben Searcy's Heirs and others. ---- The petition of Reuben Searcy, William Searcy, William Brackin in right of his wife Penelope, Jesse Searcy, Richard Searcy, James Searcy, John B. Howard, in right of his wife Harriett. William C.Rodgers in right of his wife Jane, and Charles D.McLean guardian of the minor heirs. Martin McLean deceased, Joshua Smith in right of his wife Elizabeth and James Greer guardian of the minor heirs of Susanna Greer,deceased,humbly complaining sheweth to your worshipful that on the 25 day of July 1822 a grant issued from the State of Tennessee for 5000 acres of land to Bartlett Searcy the heirs of Asa Searcy and the heirs of Reuben Searcy and their heirs that is to say Three thousand acres to Bartlett Searcy one thousand acres to Asa Searcy and one thousand acres to Reuben Searcy lying in the county of Henry and state aforesaid in the 12th surveyor's district in Range three section five on Spring Creek of fork of Obion River and butted and bounded as follows to-wit ------ Beginning at a sweet gun south 45 degrees etc. adjoining the line of John C.McLemore's 640 acre survey, etc. Gillespie's corner, etc. etc.
Your petitioner represent to your worship that the said Reuben Searcy died laving the following persons as his sole heirs and legal representatives to wit- James Searcy,

Jesse Searcy, Richard Searcy, Reuben Searoy, William Searcy,
Penelope Searcy, Harriett Searcy, Jane Searcy and Susan
Searcy, Polly Searcy, Elizabeth Searcy, Bennett Searcy and
Asa Searcy.
　　　　Your petitioner further represents that one of your
petitioners James Greer intermarried with the said Susanna
Searcy, decd and had by her in her life time nine children and
that he is entitled to one seventeenth part of 1000 acres of
land granted to the said Reuben Searcy out of the said 5000 a.
tract granted as aforesaid as guardian of said nine children,
and that the said Penelope Searcy intermarried with William
Brackin one of your petitioners and claims by virtue of said
marriage to the seventeenth part of said 1000 acres as aforesd.
And the said Jane Searcy intermarried with William C.Rodgers one
of your petitioners and claims as aforesaid by virtue of said
marriage and the said Harriet Searcy intermarried with your petitioner Jno.B. Howard and claims as heir aforesaid and the said
James Searcy, Richd Searcy, Jesse Searcy, Reuben Searoy, and
William Searcy your petitioners claim each one seventeenth part
of 1000 acres of land granted as aforesaid out of the 5000 acres
Searcy as heirs of said Reuben Searcy deceased. They further
represent that Asa Searcy one of the heirs aforesaid died leaving Elizabeth Searcy, his only heir and said Elizabeth, daughter
of said Asa afterwards married one of your petitioners Joshua
Smith who claims by virtue of said marriage one one seventeenth
part as aforesaid and that the said Bennett Searcy died leaving
one daughter as his sole heir and representative by the name of
Martio (?) (looks like Martin in another place) Searcy who married your petitioner Charles P. McLean and by him two children in
her life time and the said Charles D.McLean claims one one-seven-
teenth part of said 1000 acres of land as aforesaid as guardian
to said two children of said Martio McLean deceased.
　　　　Your petitioner further represents that they are by law
entitled to the seventeenth part specified in the manner aforesaid out of the 1000 acres that was granted to the said Reuben
Searcy deceased , and being desirous to have it laid off and set
apart to them in the manner aforesaid by butts and bounds your
petitioners have procceded and given notice to all persons interested by making publication of such their intentions in a
newspaper printed in the town of Jackson and State aforesaid as
required by statutes in such cases and provided. Henry County,
December 1825. etc.
　　　　Court held in Henry County Second Monday in December
1825 on 2nd day of said court by your petitioners to your worshipful to have commissioners appointed to set apart and lay off to
them their representatives portions out of said 1000 acres in the
said 5000 acres survey granted to the said Reuben Searcy as heirs
and legatees of Reuben Searcy, decd. etc. Signed by William C.
Rodgers, Jane Rodgers. Reuben Searcy, Wm Searcy, Penelope Brackin,
James Searcy, Harriet Howard, Richd Searcy, Wm.Brackin, Jesse
Searcy, Jno.B.Howard, James Greer, guardian of the heirs of Susanna Greer, decd.Chas D.McLean guardian for Joshua Smith & Elizabeth
Smith. Sworn to in open court by William C.Rodgers. 16 Dec. 1825.
James Hicks, clerk.

Demsey Turner and Jane Purvis are ordered by the court as administrator and administratrix of the estate of Charles Purvis, deceased. Their bond was set at $3000, etc. Jane Purvis widow and relict of Charles Purvis decd, --- lay off one years provisions for the family. 19 Dec. 1825. (C.C.Min 1825-28 p.39).

James H.Kennedy a minor orphan was released from his guardian, 19 December 1825 (C.C. Min. 1825-28, p.39).

At the court which met December 18, 1825, Robert Wade and James W.Wade Administrators of Seth Wade, deceased surrendered the administration to Samuel McGowan all the property and papers of the deceased. (C.C. Min.1825-28 p. 45).

At the court of March 6, 1826 a deed was proved from Abner Pearce, John H.Randle, James Leeper, John Stoddart and James Williams commissioners for the town of Paris to Abner Boyd for lots No.104 and 64, in said town. (C.C. Min. 1825-28 p.46).

There was a power of attorney proved from John Boon and Hannah Boon his wife, to Gabriel Moore. Court of March 1826 (C.C.Min.1825-28 p.68).

On March 8, 1826 the court proved a power of attorney from Lotty Dancer, James Dancer, Elijah Dancer, Samuel Dancer, and Thomas Dancer to John C. McLemore and General William Arnold. (C.C. Min. 1825-28 p.69).

The court of March 8, 1826 commissioners were appointed to settle with John House the administrator of George House, deceased. (C.C.Min. 1825-28 p.71.).

The November court of 1855, William Caldwell,Preston Caldwell and the Heirs of David Caldwell decd, divide the slaves of the estate. Those who signed the division - William Caldwell, Preston Caldwell, Sarah J. Smith, Eddy P.Smith, Esther A.Caldwell, William P.Caldwell, Martha Kendall, Thomas J. Kendall, Margaret Ann McNutt a minor who petitions by her guardian Elvira Caldwell VS. Ex Parte. January 10, 1856. (Co.C. Min 1849-59 , 333).

The 1856 court--- David Kendall appointed guardian to Luke M., Richard, and Mary F. and Pinkney Lee minor orphans of G.P.Lee, decd. etc. (C.C.Min 1849-59 p.356).

The July court 1856 --- Dorothy H.Kerly (Kerby) Administratrix of Benjamin G. Kerby , decd ---Rosannah R. Kerby, William E.Kerby, Sarah E.Kerby, John L. Kerby, Harriet B.Kerby, Hanah (?) O.Kerby, and Burley F.Kerby. All except Rosannah appear to have been minors. (C.C.Min. 1849-59 p.368).

At the October 9, 1856 court a petition to divide the estate, Samuel C. Edmunds, Sarah A.Edmunds, and Mary A.Edmunds, minors by next friend , heirs of John J.Edmunds deceased. There was 441 acres of land to be divided. Sarah A. Edmunds was the relict or widow and the others were the children of the deceased. (C.C Min. 1849-59 p.386.)

The August 1857 session of county court ordered Willis Cooper be appointed guardian to Joseph Cooper, minor orphan of James Cooper, deceased, and to give bond in the amount of $275,00 with N.L Lewis, James Cooper and William Cooper. securities. (C.C. Min. 1849-59 p.452).

December 5, 1836. On motion it is ordered by the court that Thomas Bowden be appointed guardian to Jackey B., Robert L., William B., Louisa J., Susan F., Thomas B., Mary F. Veazey minor orphans of Fielding L. Veaszey, deceased who thereupon entered into bond of $8000 with John Olive and James H.Howard his security (C.C.Min 1836-49 p.22).

March 6, 1837. Ordered by the court that William C. Rodgers be appointed guardian to James S., Zemrod P., Martha, Mary, John and Stephen Howard minor orphans of John B.Howard. decd, who thereupon entered into bond in the sum of $1000.00 with Swanney Burris, as his security. (C.C.Min. 1836-49 p.30).

April 3, 1837 James M.Coley, Nathan Carter and James H.Howard are appointed Commissioners to settle with Hiram Jones, the Admr. of the estate of James Jones, decd. (C. C. M. 1836-49 p.33).

John McLean Vs. Ross Skinner, case. William C.Rogers, Jacob Hoover, **Esqr.**, John H.Crutcher, William Phelps, and Aaron Winters two arbitrators to whom cause was referred and returned into court an award in the words and figures following to-wit: State of Tennessee, Sept.20th, 1823 Henry County. Undersigned arbitrators by County Court of Pleas and Quarter Session for the County of Henry to settle a matter of controversy which was pending in said court, between John McLean, Pltff. and Ross Skinner, deft. met at Moses Winters agreeable to the Commission from said court and all the parties being present, we after serious consideration found for the defendants and the plaintiff pay the cost, of suite & c. Attest: William Felps. Aaron Winters. James Hicks. etc. (Record Book A , 1824-25,p.9).

A petition regarding Patience Brake a resident of Henry County, Tenn, Wiley Brake died in Henry County July 1843 and left will probated 1843.John W.Fowler and Jesse Brake executors, refused to qualify. Henry W. **Trevathan** qualified administrator. Wiley Brake died leaving widow Patience Brake, children, Jesse Brake, Caroline Miller, Jane Brake, William Brake. Robert Brake, Catherine Robertson, wife of Duke Robertson, and John Brake his only heirs. Elizabeth Jane and William reside in Henry County, Jesse, Caroline, and John are non-residents of Tenn. Wiley Brake had property at his

death. One tract of land in Henry County in Range 5,Section
9, adjoining Hugh Bradford's entry and adjoining Pemberton's
west line 200 acres. (Enroll Book 1885-90 p.161).(This
name Brake is also found in the records written to look like
Frake.... ERW).

To the Honorable William J.Hurt, Judge of the County
Court of Henry County,presiding at Paris. Petitioners Paralee
Olive and her husband James Olive, Elizabeth C. Clevy and
husband Franklin Clevy, citizens of Henry County, Tennessee
respectfully represent to your honor that William Beyars
late of said Henry County died intestate about March 1858
leaving Margaret H.Byars heir relict and widow. Your Petitioner Paralee and Elizabeth and Missouri Byars and Mary
F. Byars are only children and heirs at law of Wm.Byard,
decd. That said Missouri and Mary F.Byars are minors under
the age of 21 years and Leroy Olive is their regular guar-
diam , that one Jas. Walker was the administrator of the
estate of William Byars deceased, that said Walker died and
Wm.F. England was appointed administrator of said Estate of
Wm. decd Byars had property. Tract of land in Henry County
one Tract 225 acres conveyed by Allen Wade . One tract about
83½ acres conveyed of D Bowden. One tract land containing
about four acres conveyed by Jesse Mandram to Wm.Byars and
one tract of 109 acres sold by decree of the County Court
and other property. etc. etc. (Enroll Book 1885- p.314).

The name Olive in Henry County, is not to be confused
with the name Oliver. They are two very distinctive families.
Petition in Court, Complainant of Samuel Olive, Ashley Olive,
I.M.H.Olive, Leroy Olive, O.C. Wagner and Icey his wife,
Martha Collier, Rebecca Stephenson, Levindes T.Olive, Arch-
ibald Phillips and Mary his wife. Jno.Churchill and Fanny
his wife, Mary Olive complainants, VS. L.Phillips, Samantha
H Phillips, Jas. Phillips, W.Jno.Phillips, Almandia Olive,
James Olive, Ann Olive, Wiley Olive, William Olive, Amanda
Olive, defendants. Orator show up July 1859 John Olive late
of Henry County departed this life intestate leaving Mary
Olive, one of your Orators, his widow and your Orator seyeth
with the Defendants his only heirs and distributees at law.
Samuel Olive and Archibald Phillips your Orator were appoint-
ed administrators of his personal estate at August Term 1859.
John Olive died possessed of property, 38 acres land in Henry
County, adjoining Joseph Olive, corner,and adjoining Dempsey
Bowden. There were some slaves. Some of the defendants are
minors. 1859-1860.signed by all of those involved. (Enroll
Book 1885- p.380).

Pleasant Diggs departed this life in Henry County,
and left a will. B. H.Diggs executor. Elizabeth Diggs widow
of P. Diggs. 4 sons and 2 daughters. Elizabeth Diggs widow
deceased recently in said county, left slaves. Order of
division of property. (Enroll Book 1885- p.14).

EARLY DEED ABSTRACTS

* * *

Hartwell Dickason of Fayette County, Tennessee, to Edmond Dumas of Henry County, Tennessee for consideration of the sum of $400 paid, conveys a tract of land in Henry County (deeds E p.41).

Jane Ritchey widow and Relict of John Ritchey, decd and Thomas J. Ritchey, William Ritchey, Samuel A. Ritchey, James M. Ritchey, Elizabeth Jane Ritchey, John M. Ritchey, and Henry C Ritchey convey to Reuben Hamilton for the sum of $1700 paid and acknowledged, a tract of land in Henry County. All sign. (E p.41).

Kelly Holliday of Henry County to A'len J. Holliday of Madison County, Tennessee, conveys all title and interest and claim to certain negroes, that belonged to Thomas Reavis decd and by him left to his wife Elizabeth Reavis by will. Refers to suit against a Lee.   2 Feb. 1835. (E.p.43).

Indenture 28 November 1832, Alexander Kirkpatrick, John W. Kirkpatrick, Samuel Kirkpatrick, William Kirkpatrick, Joseph Kirkpatrick, David Kirkpatrick, Hugh Kirkpatrick, and Paisley Kirkpatrick, sons of Samuel Kirkpatrick deceased, all of Orange County, North Carolina, except David, who is of Wilson County, Tennessee, of one part and Joseph Kirkpatrick of Wilson County, Tennessee of the other part for the sum of $40.00 assigns all claim and interest in an undivided tract of land in Henry County, Tennessee, granted by said State to Alexander Kirkpatrick decd. 317 acres. All Sign. Proved in Orange County, North Carolina. (E.p.4)

 Abner Boyd of the first part, John McLeod of the second part and John Gibbs of the third part-- Boyd is od the County of Weakley, Tennessee, and is in debt to the others mentioned. 27 May 1834 (E.p.6).

Indenture 6 January 1835, Benjamin Blythe of Henry County, Tennessee, to James Elms as guardian and agent for the heirs of John Spratte decd of Mecklenburg County, North Carolina, Interest in land 12 Surveyor's District Range 5 Section 7, on headwaters of West Sandy River it being land on which part of the town of Paris is laid off on and granted to Joseph Blythe by the State of Tennessee by Grant No._____. 20 acres. (E. p.10).

Indenture 25 Sept. 1830, Henry Brewer of Henry County, sells Elizabeth P. Wilson of Humphrey County, Tenn, for $200.00 a tract of land in Henry County on Big Sandy River, granted to Henry Brewer (could be Brawn or Brown ?) by Tennessee No.21539 Lot No.10. (E.p.13).

Indenture, James Jones of Henry County, Kemp S. Holland of Fayette County, and Samuel Kirkpatrick of Henry County, for the consideration of $1.00 paid, a tract of land in Henry County. (E.p.**22**)

Indenture 15 February 1834. Wm. W.(or M?) Hicks of Henry County,to Thomas Griffin of McNairy County, Tennessee, a tract of land in Henry County on the Fork of Obion River. (E.p.23).

Solomon Rozzell of Shelby County, Tennessee, for and in consideration of natural love and affection for my son Abshley B. Rozzell of Rutherford County, Tennessee, convey to said Ashley a ract of land 375 acres in the 12th District of Henry County on waters of North fork of Obion River. Sept. 29, 1834. (E.p.33).

Whereas the last Will of Anderson Searcy decd late of Rutherford County, Tennessee sold and divided among Beverley Randolph"s wife's children , William W.Searcey Junter's children and Robert Searcy's children, etc. Know that Lafayette Searcy one of the children of said Robert Searcy is entitled to a portion for natural love and affection for my two children Elizabeth Maury (?) Searcy and Sophia Sarah Searcy give them the interest in land and negroes in Henry County, Tenn. (E.p.37.)

22 Nov. 1834. George S.Wright admr. of James Wright, decd, for $200 sells Benj.Dunn, land in the 12th Surveyor's District,of Henry County. Range 3, Section 7. Beginning on SW corner of Grant No. 25416 issued by Tennessee to James Wright, January 27, 1827. (E. p.1)

Indenture 7 November 1834. James Kirkpatrick, Hugh Kirkpatrick and Robert Taylor and his wife Margaret Taylor all of Sumner County, Tennessee of one part and Joseph Kirkpatrick of Wilson County, Tennessee of the other part, for consideration of $333. 00 paid by the said Joseph Kirkpatrick and same acknowledged, an undivided tract of land in Henry County granted by the State of Tennessee to Alexander Kirkpatrick decd. 317 acres. (E.p.3.)

John Cooney has a fee simple interest in (said interest being 1/5 to take effect after the death of Ellen Cooney who has a life estate in same in lots No.22 and 23 in the Town of Paris, now used by Mrs. H. Lamb as a residence---- on North Depot Street on east by Brewer St and on the South by Wood S reet. 1/2 acre of land more or less for $100 paid. John Cooney and wife Jennie of Davidson County, Tenn. convey same to H.Lamb. 29 Sept. 1879.Signed John Cooney, Jennie Cooney. (U.p.492).

In consideration of one hundred Seven and 87/100 dollars paid by Henrietta Lamb to M.H. Freeman, sheriff of Henry County, I this day by this instrument transfer and

convey unto the said Henrietta Lamb all the right title
claim and interest I have in and to the following described
real estate to wit- A lot or parcel of land situated in Paris,
Henry County, Tennessee and all the appurtenances thereunto
belonging the same being known as lots Nos. 22 and 23 in the
original plan of said town the same upon which the said
Henrietta Lamb now resides and bounded as follows - on the north
by Depot Street on the east by Brewer Street on the south by
Wood Street and on the west by the alley. Feb.16, 1886. Signed
Ellen Cooney. Proved Feby 16, 1886. (X.p.474).

Henrietta Lamb, Ellen Cooney, Jno.Cooney, and wife
Gennie Cooney (Jennie Cooney), H.C.Cooney, C. Aden and T.C.
Fryer all of Henry County, Tennessee except Jno.Cooney and wife
and H.C.Cooney who are citizens of Davidson County, Tennessee,
have this day bargained and sold and do hereby transfer
and convey to W.P.Porter and J.W. Trevathan for the consideration
of twenty-five dollars to each of us paid separately all of our
right title and interest in and to the undivided tract or parcel
of land situate lying and being in the town of Paris, Tennesee.
The lot was on the Southeast corner of the Public Square in the
town of Paris, corner to R.D. Coldwell's lot, etc. the said
interest conveyed herein by C. Aden and T.C. Fryer was the former
interest of Wm. E.Cooney they jointly owning the same which is
one fourteenth and the others own one fourteenth each to have
and to hold the same to the said W T.Porter and J.W. Trevathan,
etc.   6 Dev.1879. Signed by H.C.Cooney, John Cooney, Jennie
Cooney, T.C. Fryer, Henrietta Lamb, Ellen Cooney and Clinton
Aden. Proved in Davidson County, 26 Dec. 1879. Proved in Henry
County, Dec. 31, 1879. (U. p.593 Henry Co.).

Indenture 24 May 1870 O.F.Braswell and Mary J. Bras-
well of Henry County, of one part, James T. Cooney and Charles D.
Cooney of said county of the other part, for and in consideration
$440. paid by Braswell, acknowledged , conveys to James T and
Chas. D. Cooney a part of lot No. 6 on SE corner of the Public
Square in Paris, Tenn. (Q p.750).

James W.Weldon and James E.Ratree conveyed by Charles
D. and Jas. T.Cooney Oct.21, 1868. for $10652.25. Land in Civil
District No. 15 and 20 of Henry County, .One tract begins at
the mouth of Big Sandy where it emptied into the Tennessee River
and runs up the Tennessee River. 51 degrees. Also another tract ,
etc. (Q.p.176).

Alason Powell of ____ ? County deed of gift for "love
and affection I have unto my granddaughter Martha Ann Mariah
Marshall" after the death of my wife. Refers to son Alanson.
Martha Ann not 21 years of age. Deeds negroes. Also refers to
"My daughter Priscilla Marshall", 4 Dec. 1828. Signed Alanson
Powell. Witnesses, Benjamin Peeples. Marling Peterson. (C p.1).

Samuel Hankins one of the administrators of Lucas
Kennedy, decd. of Henry Countyconveys to John Gibbs certain
negroes. 5 Feby 1828. (C.p.2.).

Alanson Powell, a deed of gift " good will and affection " to daughter Eliza Cole, Deed certain negroes. 4 Dec. 1827 (C.p.2)

Indenture, Oct. 15, 1828, Jesse Adcock 128 acres purchased from Wm.Townsend. Land in Henry County. (C.p.3)

James McGowen of Maury County, Tennessee sold Samuel McGowen of Henry County, negro girl slave. 28 Dec. 1827 (C.p.8).

Charles Neely of Calloway County,Kentucky for and in consideration of the sum of $475,00 conveys Simeon Walton of Henry County, Tenn, certain negroes. 20 May 1827. (C.p.8)

Elizabeth Bonds of Henry County, for the natural love and affection "I bear unto my beloved granddaughter" Martha Fletcher and also because said Elizabeth Bonds is moving, conveys negroes to Martha Fletcher, 28 Feby 1828. Signed Elizabeth (X) Bonds. Witnessed by Samuel McGowen and James Leeper. (C. p. 8).

Elizabeth Bonds for love and affection to granddaughter, conveys negroes to Granddaughter Juliette Wade. 28 Feb.1828 (C.p.9).

Elizabeth Bonds for love and affection to granddaughter conveys certain negro to granddaughter Harriett Wade. 28 Feb.1828 (C.p.9).

March 3, 1828, John Matthis of Trigg County, Kentucky to Daniel Matthis of Henry County, Tenn. 55 90/160 acres of land in Henry County, Tenn. (C p.12).

Bethany Kendall of Henry County, for consideration of love and good will and affection " I bear to my loving children" namely, Nancy Palmer, Sarah High, Neddy Elams Kendall Bethany Moody, William Barnett Kendall, Lurany Kendall of the county and State aforesaid and Elizabeth Rowland of Carroll County, Tennessee and John B.Kendall and Lucy Parker of Montgomery County,North Carolina, coveys that legacy that will be coming to me in North Carolina of my father's estate at my mother's death. March 3, 1828.Signed Bethany Kendall. Witnessed John Davidson, William Palmer. Henry (X) Moody. (C.p.13).

Alanson Powell for consideration of good will love and affection unto son Alanson Powell conveys certain negroes and land 150 acres in Henry County,Tenn. 29 July 1826. (C.p.16).

Indenture 24 May 1827 John Hicks attorney in fact of Nathaniel Mason Exec. of Estate of James McKee decd of the County of Franklin and State of North Carolina of one part

and Blount Cooper of the County of Henry and State of Tennessee
of the other part for the consideration of $440 paid by
Blount Cooper and same acknowledged. Tract of land in
Henry County, Tennessee. (C.p.18).

Indenture 6 June 1828, James Greer of Paris in Henry
County, to Wm.Amour and Henry Lake of Jackson, Madison County
Tennessee lots 17 and 37. (C p.26).

Indenture 3 June 1828 between Jesse James administrator of the Estate of William James decd of Henry County,
conveys to Cullen Brittain of said county 135 acres of land.
(C.p.29).

Indenture Oct.3, 1828, Nancy Ann Horton of one part
and Francissa Horton and Catroin Horton a daughter and son
of the said Nancy Ann Horton for the consideration of the
natural love and affection, conveys slaves. Signed Nancy Ann
Horton. (C.p.41).

Thomas Jones to Hartwell S.Dickason both of Maury
County,State of Tennessee, conveys 640 acres in Henry County,
Tennessee. 5 June 1826. (C.p.54).

Indenture Sept.1,1828. Between Mathew Pate and Polly
Pate daughters and heirs of Jacob Meek decd.of Washington Co.
Illinois sell Benjamin Dunlap of Henry County,Tennesee 16 2/3
acres of land in Henry County. (C.p.61).

Indenture 27 August 1828. Mary S Miller of Henry County,
conveys to Sally Pearce of said county for natural love andd
affection to daughter Salley Pearce conveys land in Henry County
Tennessee. (C. p.70).

Henry Brawn one of the Lawful heirs of Henry M. Penix
second of Henry County, 153 acres land 14 July 1828 (C.p.84).

Indenture 6 December 1828. Hiram Langston and Eleanor
Langston, daughter and heir of Jacob Meek, decd of Henry County,
to John Witt, 16 2/3 acres in Henry County, part of the land
Jacob Meek did live on. (C p.85).

Indenture 11 April 1827. Elizabeth Witenwall and
Polly Whiten (the first time is looks like Witenwall and the
second time it is clearly Whiten-- ERW) heirs of William Burges
decd of Cambden & Cartwright in the State of North Carolina ,
sells James Blackman of Sumner (likely to be Blackmore ---ERW)
County,Tenn 99½ acres in Henry County, Tenn. (C p.86).

Indenture 7 November 1828, Nathaniel H.Buckley of
Hickman County,State of Kentucky, to Benj.R. and Wm.R. Lewis of
Henry County, Tenn.100 acres land in Henry County.(C p.88).

Indenture 7 April 1828. R.K. Haley of Franklin Co. Ala.,
to John C.McLemore and James Valx of Davidson Co.Tenn.90 acres land
in Henry County. (C.p.89).

Nathaniel Norfleet for love and affection "I bear to my daughter Jacoline Norfleet" conveys slaves bought at Lewisburg, Witness Marmaduke Norfleet, William Whitefield, Robert Norfleet, and James T.Norfleet. 1828 .(C.p.92)

Indenture February 1828, David Floyd and wife Jane Floyd, formerly Jane Cathey, Cannon Taylor and his wife Matty Taylor,formerly Matty Cathey, William Vickers and his wife Rebecca formerl. Rebecca Cathey, John Robbins and his wife Polly, formerly Polly Cathey, George Cathey, and William Landers the Heirs and Legal Representatives of Andrew Cathey decd of Tennessee, of the one part to John Adkins of Henry County, Tennessee 67½ acres in Henry County, Signed by all. (C p.123)

Indenture 12 June 1829, Silas S.Stephenson of Craven County,North Carolina to Joseph L. Wilson of Wilson County, State of Tennessee 914 acres of land in Henry County, Tennessee. Part of land in Carroll County Tennessee. said land granted Heirs of Benjamin Stephenson for his service right. (C.p.126).

Francis McConnell of Henry County sold John Knowles of Barren County,Kentucky, certain negroes, Registered Oct. 9, 1829. (C.p.135)

Indenture 31 July 1829. Elisha Atkins and Joseph Atkins only heirs and representatives of William Atkins of Wythe County,Virginia convey to John C.McLemore and James Valux 100 acres in Henry County, Tenn. Valux was of Madison County, Tenn. (C.p.136).

Indenture 21 April 1829. Charles I.Love of Davidson County to Richard M.S.Love of same. 500 acres in Henry Co. Tenn. (C.p.138)

Indenture April 1, 1829 Bailey Hardeman of Williamson County, Tenn. to Howell Edwards of Henry County, 640 acres in Henry County. (C. p. 140).

Indenture, Richard Ridgeway of Weakley County, Tennessee to Reuben McGowen of Henry County, sells negroes 1829 (C.p.143).

Indenture 14 July 1827. John Marberry of Haywood County, Tennessee to David Wallace of Henry County, 150 acres in Henry County. (C p.145).

Robert Roland of Henry County for love and affection to son Clarke Roland and divers causes my etc. conveys property in Tenn. 12 Dec. 1827 (C .p.146).

Indenture 18 Nov. 1828. James Blasengame of Weakley County , 160 acres land to Robert .James (or Janes) of Henry Clunty, Land in Henry County, (C p.150).

Indenture 11 December 1828, William McCord,Senr., William McCord,Jr., James M.McCord, John C.McCord, all of Henry County, to Daniel Mason of the county of Montgomery, transaction of conveyance of land in Henry County, Tenn. (C. 151.)

Indenture, May 25, 1829, Daniel Holmes heir of Samuel Cornish of Hertford County,North Carolina, conveys to John Ray of Henry County,Tennessee, 274 acres of land in Henry County. (C.p.155).

Indenture 23 March 1808, George Lewis of Spartanburg County, South Carolina conveys to Jonathan Hampton of Rutherford County,North Carolina 1000 acres of land in Henry County, the State of Tennessee. (C.p.160).

Indenture, no date shown, Thomas Reed of Washington County, State of Missouri to Simeon Hiett of Henry County, in Tennessee. 120 acres of land in Henry County, Tennessee. (C. p.172).

Indenture 29 December 1827. Reaben (Reuben ?) Bowman of Henry County, Tennessee to Holden W.Nicholas of the State and County aforesaid. Reuben Bowman as well as for and in consideration of natural love and affection conveys to Holden W.Nicholas his son-in-law 24 acres of land in Henry County, Tenn. (NOTE: there are three or four conveyances in this same deed book between these parties...ERW). (C. p.178).

April 21, 1828, James Greer of Henry County transfers to James Cowan of Jasper County,Georgia 193 acres of land in Henry County, Tennessee. (C.p.182).

William Hays of Henry County, for and in consideration of a stipulated amount paid to John Hays of Robertson County, Tennessee, for a negro. 1 Jany 1829. (C.p.192).At the same time Minervia Hays sells negroes 1829.

Thomas Reed of Washington County, Missouri gave Power of Attorney to John H. Dunlap of Henry County,Tenn. 5 Sept. 1825. (C p.194).

Indenture 27 December 1828. Jesse Izler of Granville County,North Carolina, conveys 263 3/4 acres of land in Henry County, Tennessee to Peter Kendall of Henry County. (C p.220).

Elisha Bevill of Henry County, to my beloved children- Harrison Bevill, Mary Bevill, Lewis Bevill, Martin Bevill and Ann Bevill all of said county, for love and affection and the further consideration of $1.00 paid, conveys 80 acres of land in Henry County and other personal property. 14 Nov. 1829. (C.p 231).

Indenture, Benjamin Bird of Burke County,North Carolina

for natural love and affection to grandson Jonathan Bird, conveys a tract of land which is set apart for me as a soldier in the Revolutionary War of North Carolina. Also the interest of two deceased brothers Francis Bird and Moses Bird who departed this life at or about the conclusion of the Revolutionary War, and that Benjamin Bird being the only heir. October 12, 1810. (C.p.250).

In 1829 William Smith of Madison County, Tennessee conveyed to Wyman Sinclair of Henry County, 47 acres of land in Henry County. (C. p.253).

Andrew Provine of Carroll County, Tenn, had a transaction in Henry County. (C.p.258).

James B.Quigley of Hickman County, Kentucky is referred to in 1830 in Henry County, Tenn. (C.p.267).

On 23 October 1822 there was filed in the Supreme Court at Charlotte a Bill in equity. Thomas Hardiman, William Hardiman, Mary N. Perkins, Nancy L. Hardeman, Lavenia C. Hardiman, D. Hardiman, Sarah J.C. Hardiman, and Thomas J. Hardiman against Peter Ruff. The Defendant entered 23 Dec. 1796 to military land was for 274 acres and it was from North Carolina. No.4506. Said Ruff was then residing in Green Co. Tenn. and paid $100.00 to Stockley Donelson. etc.etc. (C.p.273).

Nathaniel Roberts of Granville County, North Carolina, on 18 August 1828 sold and conveyed to Thomas Persons of Granville County. This seems to have been a power of attorney to sell land in Tennessee, 10000 acres on Forked Deer River. (C.p.276).

Samuel Talkington of Graves County, State of Kentucky conveys 178 acres in Henry County, Tennessee to Edward Travis (C .p.286).

Indenture 12 April 1830. Jessee Meek of Beawer (Beaver (?)) County, Ohio conveys to Wm. Edwards of Henry County, Tenn. 16 3/4 acres of land in Henry County, Tenn, Said land came to him as an heir of Jacob Meek decd of Henry County. (C.p.305).

Indenture, the first day of November 1826 betwen B. P.Maclin of the first part and James Carter, Thomas K. Porter, Sperman Holland and William Porter, Junr, all of Henry County, State of Tennessee, of the second part, Witnesseth that the said party of the first part for and in consideration of the sum of $1100 to him in hand paid by the said parties of the second part, receipt whereof is hereby acknowledged and confirmed hath granted bargain sold aliened and confirmed and by these presents doth grant bargain sell etc. unto the parties of the second part and their heirs and assigns all the personal property which the said party of the first

part now owns, etc. etc. Signed B.P.Maclin, William Porter, Jr.
Witnessed by William Porter, Senr. Agnes Porter. Proved in Court
Sept. term 1827. (B.p.274).

Indenture, 1 June 1827. William Porter, Senr., of Henry
County, to James D.Porter of same for $500 paid. conveys
tranct of land in Henry County in 12th Surveyor's District,
Tennessee Grant on warrant No.823 in Sixth Section of Sixth
Range in said District on waters of Sandy River. (C.p.303)

Indenture 25 Feby 1824. Benjamin P.Maclin of the
County of Giles in the State of Tennessee of the one part and
John Atkins of Henry County. Benjamin P. Maclin for and in consideration of $1260 paid sells and conveys to John Atkins and
heirs or equal undivided fifths of a certain tract of land 225
acres in 12th Surveyor's District in the 4th Range and Seventh
Section, etc. adjoining Charles Crutchfield's entry No.125 for
304 acres, etc.by virtue of entry made in the name of Alexander
McMillen No.140 dated 12 December 1820 on which grant issued
to Alexander McMillen on No.17317 on 6 June 1822, and conveyed from said McMillen to B.P.Maclin. etc. Signed B.P.Maclin
H.W. Dunlap his attorney. Witnessed by J.W. Cook and John H.
Dunlap. Proved in Henry County, Tenn. Court 1825. (A.p.320).

Indenture 3 June 1824 Seth Wade of Randolph County,
North Carolina, Alexander Gray of the same of the second part
and Jesse Harper of the same place of the third part, regards
517½ acres land in Henry County, Tenn. Whereas John Stillwell
late of Johnson Co.N.C. departed this life intestate without
issue and administration to Eleanor W. Stillwell and Philip
Raiford by Johnson County Court and the next kin of the said
Thomas Stillwell decd sets over to Wade all their interest and.
title (A.p.305).

Robert Wade's power of attorney conveys 640 acres of
land to Seth Wade. Seth Wade of Randolph County,N.C. for divers
good causes and consideration, appoints Robert Wade of same, attorney to convey land, to contract for the locating and surveying
two military land warrants issued by the Secretary of State of
North Carolina to a man by the name of Richard Smith No.714 and
715 in West Tennessee, vacant land reserved by Congress in the
State of Tennessee for satisfying the Revolutionary Military
land claims of North Carolina, etc. (A.p.413).

Indenture 19 August 1822. Ellis Riggs of Grainger Co.,
Tenn. to Thomas Read of Henry County for and in consideration of
$750 paid. transfers land in Henry Co. (A. p. 191).

Indenture December 4,1823 R.E.C. Dougherty of Carroll
County, Tenn.260 acres conveyed to William Walters of Henry Co.
(A.p.192).

R.E.C.Dougherty of Carroll County, conveys 274 acres
of land in Henry County, to John Givins, Dec. 2, 1823 (A.p.193).

R.E.C. Doherty for divers causes and moving, appoints Samuel McCorkle of Henry County, his attorney to act, sell etc. his property in the Western District, March 13, 1824. (A.p.207).

William Kendall sells to John A.Allen on January 19, 1861 a tract of land in Henry County, Borth parties of Henry County. (O p.313).

A power of attorney April 5, 1861 Ben Kendall and John F.Kendall of the firm of Ben Kendall & Co. Reference is made to David Kendall executor of John Kendall, decd. sells Isaac M.Hudson and Jas.S. Brown. Appointed by Power of attorney to make the same. (O p.420).

H.F. Cummins to H.A. Boden, To secure note of H.P. Dunlap due 26 Feby 1870 for $335.00 etc. from firm of Cummins and Dunlap. To children of George W.Courts decd, for whom I am guardian. To secure debt. Note. H. P. Dunlap due Feb. 26, 1870 for $335. 01 and $40. due to late firm of Cummins & Dunlap, $1271 due to children of George W.Courts decd for whom I am guardian. Note due W.D.Kendall guardian for his daughter Anna Crawford for about $238. Rent due W.L. Pryor for his business house to date, now occupied by me at cut rate of $300 per annum. An account due R.C. Stevens for $150. Conveys and sell to H.A. Boden of Paris my estate, entire stock of Groceries and Merchandise now in possession at my place of business for consideration $5.00 paid. 9 May 1870. Signed H.F.Cummins. Acknowledged in Henry County, Tenn.May 9, 1870. (Q. p.723).

Indenture 1 January 1869 Between John H.Dunlap of Henry County, to Nicholas Palmer, Washington Palmer, Charles Palmer, Isaac W.Palmer, Reuben Palmer, and Leudson Palmer, of Henry County. $1240 paid, sold to Palmer, tract of land in said county 62 acres, adjoining Wm.Powell's southwest corner. Signed John.H.Dunlap.(Q.p.265).

Indenture 29 March 1841. John H.Dunlap sells Andrew Boran of same place. 210 acres of land part of grant by Tennessee to Bryant and Watson, for 400 acres of said 100 acres lines in Weakley County, 200 acres in Henry County. (G.p44).

Elizabeth Cooper of Henry County, sold to " my step-son" John T.Cooney for the use and benefit of his mother Mary Cooney, my negro boy named Manuel about four years old. Consideration of $5.00 paid, and love and affection "I" bear toward my said step-daughter Mary Cooney and my said step-grandson James T.Cooney, etc. 28th Oct.1845. Signed Elizabeth (X) Cooper. witnessed Jno.Elm Cooper. Jesse C.Cooper. (I p. 241).

Indenture 24 August 1842. Jennings H.Courts of the first part and Nathan Williams of the second part. Ann Eliza Morgan of third part, all of Henry County. Jennings H.Courts for consideration of Love and affection he has for his daught

erAnn Eliza Morgan wife of Wilie A.Morgan and being willing
and desire to secure to said Ann Eliza Morgan during her natural life the services of one negro slave and for further
consideration of the sum of $1.00 paid by Nathan Williams to
the said Jennings H.Courts hath by these presents give grant
bargain sell and deliver to the said Nathan Williams one
negro boy named Jesse about the age of 5 years and the said
Jennings H.Courts for himself and his executors doth covenant
and agree to and with the said Nathan Williams that said negro
is sound and healthy. Signed J.H.Courts. N.Williams. (G.p.318).

By virtue of authority of a power of attorney executed
by me George McNeill Courts on 7 June 1879 and Registered in
Henry County, Book U.p.490, do bargain and transfer and convey
to D.C. Crouch for $115 paid and acknowledged all interest and
claim of said George McNeill Courts in and to a tract of land
in Henry County Civil District No.16, and bounded as follows -
beginning at South west of Wm.Hayns occupant, runs west, adjoinin
Mrs. Darnell. Cross Creek, passing Wm.Haynes NW corner, estimated
118 acres. Signed James C.Courts, attorney for Geo.McNeill Courts
(U p.501).

George McNeil Courts and wife Ann Courts of Galveston,
State of Texas, empower James C. Courts of Carroll County, Tenn,
as our attorney to sell our interest in and to land in Henry
County, collect and receive all moneys due us from one .W.D.
Kendall who is now acting as trustee under a trust conveyance
formerly made to him by one James A.Courts, for the benefit of
the Estate of R.H. Crawford. Anna Courts formerly Anna Crawford.
Land in Chancery Court at Paris 7 June 1879. Signed Geo.McNeill
Courts, Anna Courts, Acknowledged Galveston, Texas 7 June
1879. Recorded in Carroll County,Tenn 24 June 1879 and recorded
in Henry County, Tenn. (U.p.490).

Know all men by these presents that we H.F.Cummins and
wife Susan M. Cummins for and in consideration for the sum of
$200 to us in hand paid receupt acknowledged have this day bar-
gained and sold and do hereby transfer and convey to George
McNeill Courts all right title claim and interest in and to the
unsold portion of a tract of land 551 acres which the late
Jennings H.Courts died seized and possessed and known as Ell
Grove a part of which was sold for division by order of Chancery Court at Paris there remains unsold 2 lots No. 3 of 62
acres and 155 poles and the older lot No.4. of 82 acres 73 poles
both lying in Henry County , etc. 12 June 1879. (U.p.405).

J.H.Courts sells Samuel W.Puckett, land for $300. paid
or secured. Land in 12th Surveyor's Dist. Range 7 Section 8,
adjoining Easleys line, 2 acres of land. 14 Aug. 1866 (Q.p.163)

Indenture 9 Dec. 1876 S.C.Cooper and wife Agnes sell Mrs. E.Bennett
for $500 a tract of land adjoining the Williams tract, in Civil
District No.14. of Henry County. Both sign. (U.p.198).

Indenture 22 Sept. 1858. James F.Smith of Benton,
County, Missouri of one part and Tandy G.Morris of Henry
County, Tenn. of other part, for $1650 paid to J.F. Smith
by T.G.Morris acknowledged, sells conveys to Morris a
tract of land in 12th Surveyor's District of Henry County,
Range 4 Section 9 on head waters of Clark's and Obion
River beginning on Southeast corner of 640 acres survey
entered in name of heirs of Dempsey Daugherty etc. 10½
acres of tract adjoining above tract in Henry County sold
by Lucius J.Polk to said James F.Smith being part of 5000
acres tract granted Thomas Polk. 54½ acres. Signed James F
Smith,Acknowledged in Benton County,Missouri Oct.19, 1858.
(N. p.470). Recorded Henry Co.Tenn.

Power of attorney.John W.Coats and wife Eliza of
Dallas County,Texas sell Samuel S.Paschall. Eliza was
formerly Elizabeth J.Johnston one of the heirs of George
Johnson decd of Henry County, Tenn. (O p.72).

Indenture 14 May 1835 Nathan Williams of Rutherford
County, Tennessee to Samuel Nelson of Henry County that
the parties having been engaged in the Mercantile Business
in the county of Henry aforesaid trading under the style
and firm of Nelson Williams and as said party of the first
part did on 24 January 1834 sell to the party of the second
all his interest in the aforesaid concern Now said party
of the first part conveys to said party of the second part
for the consideration specified in the conveyance of my
interest in said concern my interest as follows: described
tracts of land which is a part of the effects of the aforesaid concerns. one tract of land on which the said party of
the second part now resides and the same on which the aforesaid Mercantile business has been transacted lying and being in the county of Henry and State aforesaid on the
waters of Obion River in Range 5 Section 5, etc. North of
Northwest corner of Entry No.690 for 1000 acres in name of
Amos Baird, etc. 25 acres also tract land adjoining the
above containing 45 acres which is held by Entry No.2600
founded on patent of Certificate warrant No.3517 dated 21
June 1833 issued by the Secretary and Commissioner of West
Tennessee to H.L. Douglass, adjoining Southeast corner of
entry No.1996 for 25 acres. Signed Nathan Williams. Witness
T.N.Watkins, Wm.Broach. (E.p.96).

Daniel Culp of the town of Paris, Henry County,
Tenn, sells William Logan and Wm.A. Shelby of Glasgow,Bar-
ren County,Kentucky, 23 Nov. 1836, a tract of land in the
Town of Paris, Consideration Logan and Shelby securities
for Daniel Culp. The consideration being $650. Land on road
to Kentucky. Said Daniel Culp having moved to the State of
Tennessee, leaving Logan and Shelby bound to pay said $650.
Signed Daniel Culp. Proved December court 1826. (B.p.15).

James M. Culp of Barren County,Kentucky, Daniel Culp

of Henry County, Tenn. Tract of land 156 89/160 acres . Indenture
15 Dec. 1826. The consideration being $600, for two town lots in
Paris, Nos. 56 and 89. (B.p.255).

Indenture May 19, 1828. Daniel Culp of Henry County,
sells John Brown of same place 80 acres of land for a consideration
of $60.00 paid by Brown . lot no.98 in town of Paris. Signed
Daniel Culp. Witnessed Will Hilliday. Johanna Smith. (C.p.93).

EDMUNDS CO-PARTNERSHIP------ Registered Dec 16, 1837 ---
Indenture and Articles of coopertnership made and entered into
this 14 day December 1837 between Terrence Cooney and James T.
Edmunds both of Paris, Tennessee. Witnesseth, that Whereas the
said James T.Edmunds having purchased of William Arthur his interest in the property belonging to Conney & Arthur at the mouth
of Sandy the said Cooney & Edmunds do hereby mutually agree and
covenant to and with each other to form a partnership on the con-
ditions and for the purposes hereinafter expressed and for and
in consideration of the premises it is agreed that the said property consisting of the following described tracts of land viz - One
tract of 56 acres beginning at the mouth of Sandy River where it
empties into Tennessee River thence up the Tennessee South 51
degrees East 170 poles to a Stake with Hickory and Gum pointers
the Beginning corner of entry No. 751 for 640 acres made in the
name of John McIver thence due West 153 poles to a stake in the
said River Sandy the North West corner of said Entry No.751
thence down the River North 33 degrees West 50 poles thence
North 60 degrees east 90 poles to the Beginning being the same
granted by the State of Tennessee to William Arthur and by him
conveyed to James T'Edmunds.One other tract containing 160 acres
lying in Henry County immediately below the mouth of Sandy Beginning at the Mouth of Sandy where it empties into Tennessee
River at low water mark thence South 60 degrees East 80 poles
up said Sandy River to a stake thence South then degrees West
11 poles to a hickory with three black oaks and two hickorys as
pointers on the West bank of Sandy thence West 90 poles to two
Cherry Trees in a field thence North 245 poles to a stake with
one black oak pointer thence East 35 poles to an Elm on the bank
of Tennessee River thence up said River South 12 degrees east
80 poles thence south 39 degrees east 80 poles to the Beginning
being the said tract conveyed by Thomas Gray to T.Cooney and well
known as the Mouth of Sandy tract containing the Ferry Landing
& C. one other tract of 24 acres adjoining above tract of 160
acres beginning at a Double Cherry Tree and a field Southwest
corner of above 160 acres tract thence North 20 poles to a black
oak the Southwest corner of a 640 acre tract granted by the
State of Tennessee to Samuel Emmerson thence West 40 poles to
a black oak with two hickory pointers and one white oak a con-
ditional line thence South 50 poles to a stake in a field in
the North boundary line of Entry No.1523 thence East 20 poles
to its Northeast corner thence South 31 poles to a stake with
two post oak pointers thence East forty poles to a stake with
black oak pointer thence North 61 poles to a hickory with
three hickorys and three sweetgums pointers of the South
boundary line of about 160 acres tract thence West with the

same 20 poles to the Beginning, being the same tract granted
by the State of Tennessee to Terrence Cooney one other
tract lying on the West bank of Tennessee River in Henry
County containing 640 acres Beginning on the bank of the
Tennessee River at the Southeast corner of Bailey Hardeman
entry No.162 of 40 acres at an Elm with an ash and cherry
pointer, thence West with Hardeman's line 320 poles to a
persimmon tree thence South 575 poles to a black oak thence
East 180 poles to a black oak on Thomas Gray's line , thence
North with said line 182 poles to his Northwest corner
thence East 34 poles to the Tennessee River his corner thence
down the River as it meanders North 10 degrees West 100
poles to an Ironwood Thomas Gray's corner of his other
occupant thence West with his line 90 poles to a white oak
his corner thence with his line North 220 poles to a Sweet
gum his corner thence East with his lines 154 poles to a
stake on Tennessee River thence down said River as it
meanders North twenty five degrees East 78 poles to the
Beginning being the same tract granted by the State of Tennessee to Samuel Emerson and conveyed by Thomas H.Perkins to
Peters & Arthur one other tract containing 40 acres lying
on the West bank of Tennessee River adjoining above tract,
Beginning on the bank of Tennessee River at a hickory with
two Spanish Oaks and hickorys as pointers the Northeast
corner of Entry No.116 made in the name of Comer & Lane for
250 acres running thence West 58 poles to a stake and ash
with a sweetgum and hornbeam pointers thence North thirty
eight poles to a large SweetGum with an ash and hickory
pointers thence west 90 poles to a hickory with two hickory
pointers on the bank of Tennessee River thence up said River as it meanders thence South sixteen degrees West 40 poles
thence South 20 degrees West 65 poles to the Beginning the
same tract conbeyed by Alexander Brightwell to Cooney &
Arthur on which the Ferry Landing is situated one other
tract of 400 acres lying on the East bank of Tennessee in
Stewart County. Beginning on a hickory and a black gum
thence 600 to Samuel Norwoods corner on Tennessee River
thence down the River 106 poles to a stake thence South 106
poles to the beginning being part of 1000 acres purchased by
Brightwell and Lumpkins of E.B. Davidson and conveyed by A.
Brightwell to Cooney and Arthur the tract of land on which
the Ferry is situated one other tract of one acre on the
East bank of Tennessee River in Stewart County Beginning
at the Northwest corner of a tract of land bought by A.
Sexton of Lockhart where it joins James Grays land on the
bank of the Tennessee River at low water mark running with
the River and with said Lockharts and Grays line equal dis-
tances for quantity being the same acre of land bought of
said Sexton by Cooney and Arthur shall be Jointly annexed by
said Terence Cooney and James T.Edmunds in the following
proportion the said Cooney to ? an undivided interest
of 4/7 and the said James T.Edmunds an undivided interest
of 3/7 it is however agreed between the parties that they

are to carry on business at the Mouth of Sandy in partnership
under the firm and style of Cooney & Edmunds that in consideration of the personal attention which the said Edmunds
promises to pay to the business of the firm the parties are
to divide the profit arising from the business including
Ferrages warehouse charges rents and all other emoluments of
every kind derived from the business done on the place equally between them all personal property also such as stock furniture and c now belonging to or attached to the place to belong to them jointly and in equal proportion so long as James
T.Edmunds shall reside at the Tavern and keep it as a house of
entertainment for the benefit of the firm he is to be allowed
an equitable hire for any slaves he may furnish on the place.
In witness of all which the parties have hereunto set their
hands and affixed their seals the date above written.
Signed T.Cooney. James T.Edmunds. It is further agreed
between us that neither shall sell or dispose of his interest
without the consent of the other. (F.p.104)

NOTE: The above is the place called Paris Landing
which is now partly if not all, unindated in the Kentucky
Lake waters. -- ERW.

Indenture April 24, 1807. Margaret Haslin of Craven
County,North Carolina conveys to Frederick Nash of said County
and Robert Ogden of Granville County,N.C. 12500 acres in Henry
Co. Tenn. (A. p.2.).

Robert Ogden of Granville County,North Carolina
conveys and transfers to Wm.Smith of Granville County, land in
Henry County, Tenn. Oct.15, 1807. (A.p.4).

Indenture 16 April 1821. Robert Love and Thomas Love
of Haywood County, North Carolina and John Love of Buckland
(Buckingham ?) County,Virginia 3416 acres of land in Henry
County, Tennessee, lately located. (A. p. 9).

Indenture 10 April 1821 One Robert Nelson of Buncombe
County, North Carolina conveys and transfers to John Love of
the county of Buckland (Buckingham ?) County, Virginia 3133
acres of land in Henry County, Tenn. (A.p .13).

Peter Ruff, Grant No.17661. Range 5 Section 7.
Tennessee Grant. In consideration of Military service per-
formed by Peter Ruff to the State of North Carolina. Warrant
No. 4506 dated 22 December 1796 for 274 acres entered 21 Dec.
1820 by No. 404 granted tract of land in 12th District,on waters of West Sandy in Section 7 Range 5. (A.p.17).

Power of attorney, Robert Howe to Samuel Hankins,
made in Brunswick County,North Carolina 28 October 1820. (A.p.
18 .).

Indenture 5 October 1822, William Brinkley of Halifax

County, North Carolina to John C.McLemore and James
Valux of Davidson County, Tenn, 128 acres in Henry Co.,
Tenn. (A. p.32).

Explanation of the will of Hugh Williamson, decd,
of New York City and County of New York. Will provides -
Hugh Williamson of New York City; To nephew David Williamson,nephew Johnson Williamson, nephew John Niven, nephew
David Niven, and nephew Hugh Ritchie, equally divided between them the land on Obion River in Tennessee 22500
acres.   To Hugh Williamson Collins son of Josiah Collins
Junr., of Edneton, 1/3 part of land oon Aligator River in
Tyrrell County,North Carolina, which land I hold in common
with Josiah Collins, Esq., of Edenton and Josiah Collins, Jur.,
My meador and swamp in Bergen County,New Jersey and all
property in New York to be sold. My sister-in-law Charlotte
Vandn Hanvel. My wife and two infant sons Charles and John
and my two daughters Maria and Susan. To Maria Hamilton who
at my request was named Maria for my wife, my house on Barclay
Street in which she now resides. To Susan Venden Henvel I
leave $6000. To Maria Hamilton my claim of land on or near
Kenneback River in the State of Massachusetts or in Conn-
ecticut. Mr. Lannanans charge for administration on Trecothick
estate being first deducted. To pay the heirs of Charles Ward
Opthorp. To Susan Venden Henvel land on Hudson River. Refers
to " my father". Refers to certain individuals and then
refers to their mother Margaret Niven (Neven). Nephew John
Neven or Niven of near Shippenburg. His brother David Neven.
Nephew David Williamson son of my brother David and to his
brother John. To Hugh Williamson Reynolds son of my nephew Wm.
Reynolds of Rpxbury.   Caroline and Mary Williamson daughters
of my nephew Samuel Williamson. This is a very long and
detailed will. (A. p.38).

Indenture 27 October 1843. Terence Cooney of Paris,
Tenn. sells Thomas Snead of Louisville, Kentucky for $486. paid
and acknowledged a tract of land in Henry County onWest side
of Big Sandy River in Range 7 and sections 6 and 7.of the 12th
Surveyor's District. It being the 43 acres which was con-
veyed to said Cooney by James Taylor it being part of entry
No.1034 for 2560 acres of land founded on military warrant
No.747 and granted Henry Brown and J.C. McLemore agent and by
Grant No.21539 and etc. A tract of land in Henry County
adjoining the above. Also a tract granted to said Cooney by
Tennessee by Grant No.307 dated 22 Sept. 1843 etc. Signed
T.Cooney. no witnesses (H.p.27.)

Planters Bank of Tennessee deed of Trust 970 acres
of land conveyed by T.Cooney and J.T. Edmunds. Indenture Nov.
1843. Terrence Cooney and James T.Edmunds of Henry County
to Planter's Bank of Tennessee. Consideration $5.00 paid
by Planter's Bank and same acknowledged, convey said tracts
of land in Henry County. One tract of 56 acres at mouth of
Big Sandy River where it enters into the Tennessee River to

beginning corner of Entry No.751 for 640 acres in the name of
John McIver, being the same granted by this state (Tenn.) to
Wm.Arthur and by him conveyed to James T.Edmonds. One tract of
160 acres lying immediately below the mouth of Sandy River where
it emptied into the Tennessee River at low water mark being same
tract conveyed to T.Cooney by Thomas Gray containing the Ferry
Landing. One tract land 24 acres adjoining the above and granted
by the State of Tennessee to T.Cooney. One tract of 690 acres
adjoining thr above 160 acres tract and corner of 24 acre tract
and corner to Bailey Hardeman "s entry No.662 for 40 acres on
Tennessee River and adjoining Isom Wood (Ward?) on the bank of
the Tenn. River corner to 160 acre tract to T.Cooney's corner.
One tract of 40 acres on West side Tennessee River immediately
below and adjoining the last mentioned tract it being on the
north boundary of the last mentioned tract being same conveyed by
Alexr. Brightwell to Cooney & Arthur. Cooney and Edmonds (Edmonds
are indebted to the Planter's Bank of Tennessee in the sum of
$11487 as evidenced by the joint notes bearing date 15 Nov. 1843
and payable one year after date, etc. Signed T.Cooney, James T
Edmonds. Witnessed by S.M.Caldwell, John Cooney. Proved and
recorded December 1843. (H.p.38).

Know all men by these present that I John Cooney of the
County and State aforesaid have this day sold and conveyed unto
Isham G.Harris for $5.00 to me in hand paid and for consideration
after mentioned property to-wit : 1 Piano Foote, 2 Bureaus, 2
poler press. 2 carpets.1 plow & gears, 1 sorrel colt, 1½ dozen chair
1 dark gray horse 1 cow and 2 claves. 1 old ox cart. 1 Mautle
Glass. 1 Diseased Mare. 2 tables and 2 bedsteads. Table furniture,
two beds and etc. Conveyance made for the purpose of following
use and trust. Isham G.Harris is Indebted to 1 Isham Boyce in the
sum of $200 due by account it being the balance due Boyce for his
negro boy Sam for 3 years, also to Blont Cooper by note due in the
sum of $125 due by note 25 Dec. 1844. One J.C.Cooper who has
become my surety in debt of $118 to the Estate of Samuel Waddy,
decd, due about 1 January 1840 upon which debt there is now a
judgement against said Cooper for debt interest and cost. Also one
Jesse C.Cooper became my security in debt to the Administration
Mrs. Williams estate for the sum of $52 by note due 15 August 1844,
being desirous to secure payment of the debt to the said Isham
Boyce and the said Blount Cooper and also secure payment of said
debts to the administrator of the estate of the said Samuel Waddy,
decd, and thereby save himself of my said surety in said debt
make certain payment to the administator of the said Williams,
deceased, etc. Cooney to keep said property in possession for
eighteen months. If debts are paid this conveyance is void. Isham
G.Harris is made trustee. etc.Sept. 6, 1844. Signed J.Cooney,
No witnesses . (H.p.194).

George McNeill Courts and wife Anna Courts convey to
James C.McNeill for $450.62, all interest and claim in and to
the estate and personal property of R.R.Crawford ,decd, in the
firm of Crawford McNeill & Co., doing business in Paris. Town lots
15 and 36 on which a large brick store house now occupied

by McNeill Brothers.   30 April 1877. (V.p.271).

      For the consideration of $2000 paid by J.L.
Lemonds receipt of which I, Marietta Dunlap Executrix of
the last will and Testament of John H.Dunlap, decd. by
virtue of authority in me vested by said Will, sell to
J.L.Lemonds several tracts of land in Henry County in
Civil District No.1. adjoining said Lemonds in 1881 and
adjoining Lemonds home tract adjoining Nat. Curruer's SE
corner. Feb.15, 1882. Signed Marietta Dunlap. (V.p.535).

      Articles of agreement entered into between Nathaniel
Currier, James C.Currier, and Terrence Cooney all of Henry
County, Tennessee, that parties on making a settlement of
the affairs of Chickasaw Cotton Factory which they have
heretofore conducted in partnership---- It appearing that
said Cooney received from said business $7404.75 and that
James C.Currier received $7705.23, Nathaniel Currier re-
ceived $1018.90, It is agreed that Cooney shall receive no
more of the profits on avails of said Factory in any way until it shall clear itsself of debt and pay to said Nathaniel
and James C.Currier enough to make the difference with legal
interest. The partnership is dissolved after Cooney pays his
equal part then he to receive his equal one third part that
might avail. 10 May 1846. Signed   , Nethal Currier,
James C.Currier, T.Cooney, " I hereby transfer to Nathaniel
and James C.Currier for value received all my right title
interest and claim in and to the property designated in the
foregoing and claim under and to the property, aforesaid
articles of agreement and relinquish all claim to same
Aug. 7, 1866. Signed T.Cooney. (P.p.267).

      Indenture 14 August 1866. J.H.Courts of Henry County
to Thomas E.Bond and Jacob Dice for consideration of $200
paid sell convey and grant unto T.E.Bond and J.Dice lot
supposed to be one acre including the Tobacco Factory and
old Grocery House in Henry County in the 12th Surveyor's
District Range 7 Section 8. First begining at SE corner of
a 2 acre tract of land deeded by John Kendall to J.F. Kendall
on which the store house of the said T.E.Bond and J.Dice now
stands and adjoining Easley's fence, including the Tobacco
Factory. Signed J.H. Courts, Witnesses. Jas. A.Courts, S.W.
Puckett. (P. p.300).

      Title Bond, John Cooney 18 Dec. 1866 bind myself in
the sum of $600 conditioned Wm.N.Griffin has purchased for
the sum of $400, etc. a lot in Paris No.4. The North part of
town. If cuase to make W.N.Griffin a good and valid title
to said lot after his paying said note of $250.00 then this
obligation to be void. Signed B.F.Lamb. Test.T.Cooney. (P.
p.412).

      Indenture 26 August 1867 John Cooney of Nashville,
and Wm.N. Griffin of Paris for the consideration of $450.00
paid by said Griffin to said Cooney, Cooney conveys in the

Northern part of Paris No.4. about 1 quarter of an acre, and adjoining on the south by McFarland and Guthrey's lot No.3. and on west by J.B.Bowden's lot No. 5, conveyed by M.P. Chandler and Wm.N. Martin to said Cooney. Signed John Cooney. Witness ; W.E. Cooney, Jas. T.Cooney. (P. p.714).

John McCrory and Elizabeth D. McRorey **formerly** Elizabeth D.Carroll to John L. Perry. Conveys land which was granted to John Carroll now deceased. 31 May 1867 (P. p.578).

H.F.Cummins and Sue M.Cummins convey to George W. Armour (Annorer?) a tract of land in said county of Henry adjoining the corner of Sarah Asborn's tract containing 30 acres. Be it understood that 10 acres 85 poles excluded have been conveyed to George W. Amoru (?) on 7 Feby 1870 . Signed by H.F. and Sue M. Cummins. (R. p. 463).

S.C. Cooper , M. A. Cooper, Tabitha Sallie Bradley, as heirs of D.C. Bradley decd, have agreed that the land should remain as stated in the Will of said Bradley. We agreed that Tabitha Bradley shall have buearu, two Bedsteads , cooking stove one scrrel mare and one yearling, waggon and Buggy, and other items. S.C.Cooper and M.A. Cooper and they to receive certain things and provisions made for them from the estate. Cooper to take care of the debt against the estate. August 9, 1871. (R. p.548).

James T.Dunlap. No.26. 133 acres at $1.62 acres. (Land Entries Book A. p.10).

Dunlap and others for Clear Creek Meeting House, No. 77, 37½ cents paid. Allen Dunlap, John M.Alexander, and Thomas Withorington as trustees for Clear Creek Baptist Church and Commissioners for School House enter 3 acres Aug.10, 1843 (Land Entries Book A. p. 29).

Terrence Cooney assignee of James Taylor by virtue of $25 paid enters 200 acres of occupancy land Range 7, Section 6 and 7. beginning east line of entry No.1034 for 2560 acres in name of Henry Brown and John C McLemore. Aug. 26, 1843.Joel Hagler, locator. (Land Entries Book A. p.17 No.47).

T. Cooney enters 134½ acres. $16.81½ paid. In Range 5, Section 7, Southwest corner of entry No.997 for 5000 acres in the name of Wm.Polk. May 24, 1844. Joel Hagler locator. (Land Entries Book A. No.85. p. 32).

T.Cooney, 115½ acres $14.43 3/4 paid Range 7, Section 7. Waters of West Sandy and Holly fork, adjoining a tract of 120 acres in name of John McIver. Dec. , 1845. (Land Entries Book A p.75. No.189).

T.Cooney enters 134½ acres $16.40. Range 6, Section 7, SE corner of entry No.101 for 59 acres in name of J.C. Narund. Dec. 4, 1845. (Land Entries Book A. p.76 No 190).

James Cooper 67½ acres $8.43 3/4. Range 5, Sec. 6, on west Sandy, adjoining John Babbs, June 27, 1846. (Land Entries Book A. page 179. No.441).

Mary Cooper, enters 90 acres $11.25. Range 4 Sec. 5 SW corner. June 30,1846. (Land Entries Book A p.214.No 527.).

The heirs of Moses Olive, enter 186 acres, Range 7, Section 10. on Cypress Creek. (Land Entries A. p.450. No.1013).

Jesse Oliver also made an entry about the same time.

Nathaniel Porter entered 31½ acres $3.93 3/4 paid. Range 6, Section 6, and 7, SW corner of entry No.606 for 300 acres in name of D.Low. Aug. 15, 1842. Said Nathaniel Porter was the locator. (Land Entries A.p.17 No.48).

The Heirs of Wm.Porter made entry in the same manner No.780 (Land Entries A.p.319).

Nathaniel Porter also made entries No.735, and 1256 and others. (Land Entries A. p.299, 517, and 401.)

James D.Porter made several entries No.156, 157, and others, as shown in Land Entries Book A pages 61 and etc.

John C.Porter's Executors made an entry which is Number 162 in Land Entries Book A page 64.

Ephraim Williams heirs made an entry No.185 as shown in Entries for Land book A page 75.

Edmonds and Cooney made an entry of 30 acres in Range 8, Section 9, adjoining James Gray on the NE corner for 160 acres January 5, 1850. (Land Entries Book A p.511).

James T.Edmonds, entered 65 acres of land $8.12½ paid Range 7, and 8 and Section 9. on Bank of Sandy River SE corner entry No.30 for 160 acres in name of Thomas Gray.March 16, 1844 (Land Entries Book A. p. 29. No.79).

Whereas Nathan Williams, Sr. died leaving a last Will and Testament in which he appointed Jennings H. Courts, Francis Williams and Nathan Williams, Jr., his executors, which will was admitted to probate in and before the County Court of Henry County and the said Francis and Nathan Williams have since died and whereas I, Jennings H. Courts the Sole and Surviving Executor of the Last Will and Testament of Nathan Williams, Sr. decd, have heretofore to act on or about the 8th day of June 1838 by virtue of the authority

vested in me by the said last will and testament, sold and do
transfer and convey unto Wilie A.Morgan and his heirs for the
consideration of $1000 and to secure the payment of which the
said Wilie A.Morgan executed his three several promisary notes
each for $333.1/3 dated 8 day June 1838 one of which notes is
due the first of January 1859 and one due 1st day of January
1860 and one due the first day of January 1861 an' each of said
notes is under seal with John M. Williams security on each of
them. Oct.31, 1859. J.H.Courts, Surety Exec of Nathaniel
Williams, decd. (N.p.826).

Jennings H.Courts of the County of Henry and State of
Tennessee for love and affection I entertain for my daughter
Frances M.Parker wife of William J. Parker and for the further
consideration of $5.00 to me paid by William H.Courts of the
County and State aforesaid, receipt acknowledged, sell and convey
unto Wm.H.Courts as Trustee for the sole and separate use of my
daughter Frances M.Parker wife of the said Wm.Parker during her
natural life and at her death to go to her children and the issue
living, etc. A tract of land in Henry County,on waters of West
Sandy in Civil District No. 6 Range 7, Section 7. Adjoining D.
'asons entry for 50 acres. Certain negroes also included in
the transaction. 29 July 1859. Signed J.H.Courts. (N.p.560).

Indenture 22 May 1856, Terence Cooney and James T.
Edmunds of one part and K.H.Caplinger of the other part. The
said Cooney being of Henry County and Edmunds now of Louisville,
Kentucky and Caplinger of Benton County, Tenn, Witnesseth that
for and in consideration of $2000 paid and acknowledged by Cooney
and Edmunds sell to K.H.Caplinger a tract of land in Henry County,
Tennessee in Range 8 Section 8 near Tennessee River which land was
granted John Swayne by the State of Tennessee Grant No.8074 dated
1 May 1849, at the NW corner of entry No.275 for 274 acres in name
of Eli Cherry on the south line of entry No.166 for 640 acres in
the name of Thomas Gray etc. Excluding 50 acres John Swayne .
Signed T.Cooney by his attorney in fact John Cooney Jr. (M. p.354).

Indenture 25 Dec. 1856 Terence Cooney to Benj.C.Brown
one tract of land 200 acres Range 7, Sec. 7, adjoining Samuel S.
Medlock and others. (M. p.464).

Edmond B.Cooper, Jesse C.Cooper, and Jno W.Cooper, the
executors of Blount Cooper decd, convey to Vernon B. Walker for
the consideration of $536 paid , by Walker, land in Henry County
on waters of Sandy in the 12th Survey's District Section 8,Range
6, adjoining on which Walker now lives. Adjoining the West corner
of the Mt.Vista tract of 96 acres. Also another tract out of Mt.
Vista tract 192½ poles doe SW corner 10 acres. Out of the first
tract of 96 acres deduct 5 acres 80 poles deeded to Walker and
Hanly. Signed E.B.Cooper, Jesse C.Cooper, J.W.Cooper. 2 May 1857.
(N.p. 588).

Another deed made by the same parties as above, as
executors of Blount Cooper, decd. conveys to Frances M.Bunch,

for 107 acres in Surveyor's District 12 Section 8, Range
6, on waters of Sandy, adjoining Solomon Copeland, and
Goodman's corner, also corner to Zadock McLester, excluding 106 acres of land which were sold to Vernon B.
Walker. etc. (M. p.489).

John M.Williams of Henry County conveys to Jennings H.Courts for $400 paid and acknowledged , conveys
interest in land belonging to the Estate of Nathan Williams
Jr, decd. in Henry County, known as Samuel Edney Tract of land.
245 acres. This for only MY portion as one of the heirs of
the said Nathan Williams Jr. deceased, estate. Releases all
claim. Signed John M.Williams. 4 April 1854. (L.p.219).

Indenture 17 March 1854 Terence Cooney conveys to
Miles P.Chandler both of Parish (Paris) for $300 paid,
a town lot in Paris No.85 same conveyed to said Cooney by
Nathaniel Crockett, 15 July 1839. (L.p.283).

Indenture June 10, 1854, Terence Cooney and John
Cooney Jr, sell to John L.Hagler, for the consideration of
$1320 to secure Hagler in payment of a note to Cooney,
mortgage negroes and hald lot on the Public Square in
Paris adjoining the store lot of Jesse C.Cooper & Co.
etc. being the 60 acres bought of John Cooney Jr, of Thos.
W. Crawford. 200 acres in Dist. 6. granted Terence
Cooney the occupant entry of which he bought of Lewis
Brown adjoining John Hopton and others. Also tract of land
granted Terence Cooney in District 6, in the bottom of West
Sandy below Copeland's old Mill and near the late residence
of the late James Parker 135 acres. Signed T.Cooney,
John Cooney Jr. (L.p.319).

Indenture 18 Novmber 1854 Terence Cooney to John
Cooney Jr, of Paris, for $4500 paid. sells John Cooney
lot No.22 and Lot No.23.in Paris, being the dwelling
house and garden usually occupied by Terrence Cooney and
now by said John Cooney Jr, and lot No. 44 being the
stable lot attached to the residence and S.O.West of it
as it crosses the street etc. (L.p.428).

Know all men by these presents that I,John Cooney,
Junior have bargained given sold and conveyed and by these
presents do convey to William Arthur of Holly Springs,
Mississippi in Trust for the use and benefit of my mother
Eliza Jane Cooney and in consideration of the sum of $1.00
and of the love and affection I bear my mother, conveys
certain slaves. 3 January 1855 , Signed John Cooney Jr.
(L. p.467).

H.F.Cummins was Mayor of Paris 31 March 1852,
The Mayor and Aldermen of Paris sell Terrence Cooney for
$7.50 and by consent of the owners, of adjoining lots.
all that alley land laid out in the original plan of the
town, between lots 22 and 23. (K.p.61).

Know all by these presents 18 Dec.1837 James T. Edmonds executed a deed of trust or Mortgage on a tract of land in Henry County at the Mouth of Sandy to secure notes , Payment was satisfied 2 Oct. 1852. Signed Will Arthur. Witnessed by T. Cooney and John Cooney. (K p.279).

John Cooney transfers to Terrance Cooney all the right, interest, he has or may acquire in the estate of his father-in-law Blount Cooper by virtue of his will duly admitted to record in Henry County, or by virtue of my administration upon the estate of my deceased wife Mary Cooney . This transfer is made to enable Terence Cooney to satisfy a note of six hundred and odd dollars that he executed to E.B.Cooper in the cause of the year 1849 or 50. Should there be any residue left in the lands of the said Terence Cooney after that object is accomplished it is to belong to the said John Cooney. 4 June 1858. (K. p.257).

This indenture made and entered into the 16 March 1849 between Hiram F.Cummins of Henry County, Tennessee of the one part and Eliza Jane Cummins and John H.Dunlap of the other part. Witness that the said Hiram F.Cummins having sold to Michael Arthur of Clay Co.Missouri an interest in a tract of land in said County of Clay and near to or adjoining the Town of Liberty in said State of Missouri and also an interest in a negro woman for $550 which said interest in said negro woman was sold to said Arthur was the property of my wife Eliza Jane Cummins by decent from her father Richard Stevens and having vested the proceeds of the said sale. etc. (J.141).

Whereas Uriah Akers have a fee simple interest in the Remainder to take effect and be with possession after the death of my mother Lucindy Akers who has a life estate in same in a tract of land in Henry County, Tennessee, District 8, 174 acres in Range 5 Section 5, for $200 paid sell to Orlanda E.Muzzel my interest, 17 Sept. 1855. (L. p.688.)

March 1,1855 Abner Akers sells to William Perkins for $800 a tract of land in Henry County, Section 5 Range 5. (L.p.683)

The following listing of deeds are brief but are helpful to those who are tracing their lineages in this section of the State of Tennessee.

David Couch deeded to Jesse C. Garner, 50 acres of land which deed is recorded in Book D page 441. O.B. Crouch deeded to Joseph Scott, 20 acres of land, recorded in Deed Book L.p.324. F.M. Crouch deeded William Williams 130 acres which is recorded in Deeds S page 6. Obadiah Crouch and wife deeded to Andrew Crouch 64 acres, recorded Book U page 787.

James Humphrey made a number of deeds in the early days of the county. He deeded Wm.Rosee 62½ acres as recorded in book D page 389. James Humphrey also deeded to Noah Hampton 1000 acres and same is recorded in Book B page 456. He deeded to John P

Pierce 50 acres of land, the same recorded in book
D page 49.

Nicholas Hale conveyed to John Jones 50 acres of
land, same being recorded in Book D page 521. He also
conveyed to Zibia H. Williams, 67 acres which is recorded
in Book F page 394.

Thomas Humphreys made a deed to R. A. Kingkendall
for 132¾ acres, same recorded in Book H page 568. He
also transferred to R.D.Caldwell 2 acres of land which
is found in Deed Book J page 220.

Martha, Horatio, Henry, Abner, Jas. G., J. P.,
Samuel, W. D., John C., and others by the name Humphreys
all executed deeds before 1883 in the county.

William Polk of North Carolina transferred lands
to Wm. Crawford in the amount of 50 acres; To John Marberry
in the amount of 440 acres; To John N.Jackson in the amount
of 500 acres; and to Peter Snider in the amount of 250
acres all before the year 1825. (Deeds A.pp.206,449,451,
524.).

Later deeds made by William Polk include; 69 acres
to Champion Terry; 148 acres to Wm. Young; 120 acres to
Hartwell S.Dickerson. (Deeds C. pp.157,302,329); Also
89 acres to Thomas Hallemon (Deeds B p.80), and 154 32/160
acres to Wm.Henry. (C.p.35). Later he deeded 250 acres
to John Barnett, and another 250 acres to Edwin Motley,
(D. 2,291).

James K. Polk deeded 68½ acres to John H.Warren which
is recorded in Book E page 179. James K. Polk gave a power
of attorney to John H. Dunlap to transact business (F page
17). Sarah Polk made many deeds before 1883 in Henry County,
which included 600 acres of land to A.R.Newport;100 acres
to Joseph Betterworth; 200 acres to James Scoggins; 150
acres to Joshua Hale; 476 acres to Wm.Collins; 512½ acres
to Richard Wright; 250 acres to Wm.Hill; 300 acres to
Andrew W.Carson; and 250 acres to James Dinwiddie. (E.pp.
223, 224, 253, 370, 371, 372, 470,. and F.p. 19).

The polks had a vast amount of land in this county,
at a very early date. Lucian,Lucius J., Leonidas and William
made transactions before 1848 and later.

Lucius J. Polk deeded to the Commissioners of
Conyersville Academy a lot about 1847 (I.p.184). Lucius
Polk deeded 5 acres of land to the Cumberland Presbyterian
Church about 1848 (I.p.415).

Some of the very early names found on the tax lists
without land in 1827 were Christly Couch, Henry Humphrey,
William W. Horn, Nathan Hale, S.George Phillips, William
Phillips, and many others. Goodloe Warren was there but

he had no land. Stephen was there and was taxed with 87¾ acres of land., while John Warren is shown with 200 acres of land. Isaac Akers had only 25 acres of land in 1827. John Bell was taxed with 320 acres in Range 4, Section 59 part of 640 acres.

In 1828 the Polks were still possibly the largest tax payers so far as land tax was concerned.-- William Poke (Polk?) no land 1 poll, 1 slave; William Polk 433¾ acres, 322 entered on a grant, in Range 5 Section 5; Thomas Polk with 4500 acres, Grant 620. Range 5, Section 6, part of 5000 acres; William Polk again with 2450 acres on grant or entry No 997, part of 5000 acre tract; Polk and Devereaux as partners had 500 acres Entry No.18, in Range 4 Section 9, and another tract or entry of 500 acres Entered on No. 47. in Range 3,4 Section 9: Samuel Polk heirs had 265½ acres part of Amos Birds 1000 acres on Entry No.690.

In the same year 1828, William Wimberly and Lewis Wimberly each had 32½ acres.

The Tax list of 1829 continues to show that the Polks owned much land in the county. Joshua Hale shows up with 30 acres and Nicholas Hale appears without land but with 1 poll.

In 1829 John Wimberly is taxed with 83 1/3 acres and 1 poll; Anthony, Henry, and William Wimberly are shown, but only William is charged with any land. He had 37½ acres, in Range 7, Section 6. There evidently were two persons named Lewis Wimberly in 1829 for there are two entries one without land but 1 poll,and the other with 57½ acres of land and one poll.

In the tax list of 1831 John Venable appears with 166 2/3 acres of land.

The Tax list of 1832 shows that the Thomas Arnold heirs had 640 acres of land, and Asheles Sneed heirs had 1752 acres.

==

Dots and Dashes

W.T.Nance came from Holmes County,Mississippi to Henry County,Tenn. He was born February 1,1842, the son of W.F. and Elizabeth (Hill) Nance. W.F.Nance was born in North Carolina April 7,1814 and came to Tennessee when about seventeen years of age, lived for a time in Rutherford County and later in Henry County,Tenn. They evidently were in Mississippi for a short period of time before settling in Henry County.

Dr. S.H. Caldwell was born December 10,1836 near Paris, in Henry County, the son of R. H. Caldwell.

J.W. Buchanan was born in the 22nd District of Henry County,June 23, 1830 son of Thomas and E. Buchanan,both natives of North Carolina,Edgecombe County,and both born about 1812.

Luke Tipton came to Henry County from Maryland where he was born,but he was in Ohio for a short time before settling here.

WHERE WERE THEY IN 1827

*   *   *

NOTE: "The West Tennessean", a newspaper published in Paris, Henry County, Tennessee, by
W. Terrill, dated Nov. 5, 1827, carried the
Message of Sam Houston, Governor of Tennessee
delivered October 15,1827. It also carried
a list of letters remaining in the post office
at Paris on the first of October 1827, un-
claimed. Those whose names appear on the list
had either been in the county and left or had
not arrived in the county. They may not have
been in Paris, but somewhere in that section
of the State.

Apperson, Peter	Barns, Charles 2
Alexander, M.	Bays, A.
Allen, Rob	Blythe, John
Alexander, Wm.	Bushart, Jacob
Allen, John	Byurs, George
Anderson, Thomas	
Aker, Isaac	Crocket, N.
Adams, Harmon	Cooke, J. W. 4
Allen, Edward	Coats, Samuel
Alexander, Anderson	Cross, Wm. 2
Allen, Amanda	Coats, Ben 2
	Crocket, J. W.
Bagg, Wm. H.	Caldwell, Rob 2
Binford, Thomas	Carter, Nathan
Beard, Rich	Cheatham, Jno.
Ballard, J. H.	Cobren, Peter
Baldwin, Lewis 2	Cooley, Elizabeth
Beard, A. M. 2	Crittenden, John
Burges, Wm.	Camthem, C.
Brown, Jeremiah 2	Crawford, Wm.
Bean, Mrs. John	Chapman, Thomas
Blount, Wilie	Carter, James 3
Bailey, Arch 2	Carson, Wm. H.
Brien, Jos. H.	Caldwell, Henry
Banch, G.	Carson, Mrs. Mary
Bynum, C. P.	Chambers, James
Bean, John	Chapman, G. G.
Boon, John	Carr, Silas
Bone, Levi	Cooke, James
Beason, Saml	Creed, E.
Brumfield, R. B.	Coats, Jesse
Boman, Wm.	Campbell, E.
Buren, Thomas	Campbell, W. H.
Buckley, James	Castle, John
Blackstone, Y.	Cockrum, Rob
Bethel, T.	
Burns, Asa	Davis, Ben

Dickey, Wm. R.
Dunn, H. W.
Ferlon, J. H.
Dunsas, Jeremiah
Dunwiddie, J. J.
Daniel, Thos. L.
Deloach, Thomas
Dement, A.

Floyd, Thos. L.
Ford, Wm. H.
Fitzgerald, Wm.
Fraker, Elias B.
Fulbright, Jno.
Furgerson, John H.
Foster, Franklin
Fields, Ambrose
Finn, John
Freeman, D. B.
Fimson, James

Gray, Thos. 4
Grayham, E. L.
Ginnings, John 2
Gill, Thos. H.
Goodwin, Jesse
Gregory, George
Greer, Isaac
Gainer, James C.
Geam, Wm.
Griffin, Cannon

Hunt, Johnanthan
Hinson, John
Holland, S.
Hutchins, Thos.
Holliday, K.
Herrin, B.
Harton, John
Harris, Samuel
Hamilton, Mrs. M.
Huntsman, John
Hayne, Wm. 2
Harper, F. W.
Hose, John B.
Haraval, Warner
Harris, Wm. R.
Holteman, Thos.
Harpoole, Daniel
Hanson, John
Hall, L. S.
Harper, F.
Holingsworth, G.
Herring, Stephen
Harding, H. W.

Hogan, Wm. G.
Hoshil, Bennet

Irwin, James

Jackson, James 3
Jennings, T. J.
Jettan, Asa
James, T. W.
Jones, James 2
James, John
Jackson, Collins

Keys, Hamilton
Knuckols, John
King, David
Knackols, Wm. 2
King, John R.

Lee, G. P.
Latta, James
Love, John D. 2
Lewis, Sam
Lewis, R. N.
Lyon, Wm.
Lester, R.
Lyon, John
Latta, A. A.
Logan, Henry

McRoberts, H.
Milton, John 2
Montgomery, A.
Matthews, Jesse
McLean, G. 2
McAdoo, Evans
McConnel, F.
McCorkle, L.
Morns, Wm.
McClure, J. W.
Mans, John
Milrany, Jos.
Moran, J. H.
Massy, Wm.
Moore, Richard
Mandy, G.
McGowan, S.
Mathense, Collins

Olive, John
Oliver, George

Parham, F.
Perkins, A.
Page, John

Pouder, N.
Peeples, Ben
Powell, Allison
Palmere, John
Powel, Wm.
Prewitt, Levi
Pemberton, John
Palmore, Wm.
Pemberton, Wm.
Poe, Joseph
Pattebone, Luke
Pike, Samuel
Patterson, John

Robertson, Wm.
Reeds, James F.   3
Reves, Thos.
Ramsey, Robert
Raney, Isaac
Rose, Kindred
Reed, James
Russel, E. E.
Russel, Furges
Robins, Charles
Richeson, J.
Ramsey, Wm.
Rusany, M.

Stone, Wm.
Sims, Nicholas   2
Seawright, Alex
Sinclear, Wayman
Smith, Jno.
Sloo, H. T.
Sulavan, Jacob
Small, Robert
Stone, R. J.
Shaw, Wm.
Snell, Stephen

Tannehill, A.   2
Taylor, Isaac
Talkington, Joseph
Thomson, Wm.   2
Trousdale, James
Turner, Wm. C.
Trantham, Flay
Turpin, S.
Townsend, J. B.
Trice, N. S.
Taylor, Wm.
Traylor, Willis

Ury, Joseph

William, R. D.
Wade, Rob
Watkins, J. H.
Watkins, James
Webb, Jourden
Wilkinson, Arch
Ward, M.
Walker, Duct ?
Wade, Wm.
Whitfield, Wm. B.
Wilson, Mrs. P.   2
Wyatt, Z.
Willis, James
Wood, John D.
Willas, John
Wimberly, Lewis
Waine, N.
Welch, Henry
Watson, Ben G.
Wade, Wm. and E.
Williams, Samuel
Webb, Johnson
Wanack, James

Young, V. John   2
Young, Jno.
Young, Mrs. Sally

Signed by the Postmaster

John L. Allen.

Note: A goodly number of these
people turn up in the
deeds recorded in the
county, at a date near
this date. --ERW

LEGISLATIVE PETITIONS

Note: The following is a list of Petitions
filed in the General Assembly of the
State of Tennessee, in the early years.
The petitions frequently contain most
valuable information in regard to the
development of the county, and often
regarding individuals. A good number of
the petitions have long lists of signatures. These are original signatures
of the individuals. The original petitions are on file in the Tennessee
State Archives at Nashville. They are
very fragile,but can be duplicated in
most instances. ERW.

Year Presented	Subject
1821	Commission for bridge across Duck River.
1822	Sandy River, Mill Dam.
1823	Thomas Gray refund.
1823	Rich Anderson dam on Duck River.
1823	Derinda Stone ask for divorce.
1825	Citizens to work road.
1826	Edwd Stringer, for Justice of Peace.
1826	Jos. Curtis, to sell liquor without a license.
1829	Building a Courthouse
1831	Wm. Bailey compesation for slave killing.
1831	N. P. White, ask divorce.
1831	Justice of Peace compensation
1833	Ferry at Perryville
1833	Regards Bridge
1837	Repeal navigation of Big Sandy River
1837	Regards Tennessee River to Kentucky Line.

1837   Petition of protest certain etc.

1837   Petition regards jail and courthouse in the County.

1837   Petition regards Chancery Court at Paris or Dresden

1829   Kemp.G.Holland, Tax Collector appointed for County.

1822   James Jones named Circuit Court Clerk of the County

1827   Ann Swisher asking for divorce.

1821   Asking to exempt from taxation,five acres of land
on Bird's Creek, on which Bird's Creek Meeting
House now stands (Baptist).

1832   Petition to erect saw and grist mill on Crooked
Neck Mill Creek.

1837   Petition, citizens of Henry and Benton Counties
asking that the Big Sandy River be declared not
navigable.

1839   Petition regarding Tippling Law.

1841   Commanding officers of the 114th and 115th Regiments
asking the establishment of the present mode of
Regimental Drills.

1841   Members of the Bar in the 9th Judicial Circuit of
the State of Tennessee asking to alter the session
of the Circuit courts in said county, so as to be
two-term annually.

1841   Asking to repeal the Act of 1829, on the subject of
Public Nusiances.

1841   Asking an appropriation for the purpose of clearing
out Obion River.

1842   Petition relating to Mill Dams

1842   Lewis Brown asks to sell liquor without a license

1842   Petition from Henry, Carroll, Weakley counties to
open the Obion River.

1843   Juncey C.Quinn ask to be made femi-sol. Refers to
her father as a soldier in some war but does not
give his name or which war.

1847   Josiah Alderson, to hawk and peddle.

1847   Asking that the corporate limits be extended,Paris.

1845   Relief of Francis Copeland in re-land claim.

----   No date shown. Petition Zachariah Noel to free slaves.

1853   Certificates of election for the members of the leg-
         islature from the county. (These are found for most
         of the years and listed only once here. They cover
         the certifications of the election of Representatives
         and Senators.). In 1853 William E. Travis, Owen H.
         Edwards, L. M. Thorpe and H. F. Cummigs were elected
         to the house and James F. Dunlap and John A. Gard-
         ner to the State Senate.
         In 1857 Jonathan J. Lamb and James D. Porter were
         elected to the State Legislature. In 1865-66 Nath-
         aniel Porter and Joseph H. Travis were elected to
         the State Legislature. etc. etc.

1855   Jas. A. Cannon, ask for divorce.

===

DOTS AND DASHES

        There was a lawsuit, Simpson Alexander VS G.R. Man-
ley, et als, Ex Parte, Petition filed July 7,1856. The administrator of the estate of W.H. R. Alexander was appointed
September 1854. Bond was entered according to law. There were
numerous debts owing to said estate. Possession was mentioned
of a house and lot in the town of Caladonia. One half of another
house and lot in Caladonia and some slaves are also mentioned.
W.H.R. Alexander left a widow Lucretia who after his death in-
ter-married with one G.P. Manley, and an only child named Martha that said widow and her husband had are all three citizens
of Henry County. The said Lucretia is entitled to dower in
said property,etc. W.H.R. Alexander died in 1854. (Henry
County Docket 1870-85 p.51.)

        Cooper Postlewaite et al and heirs of Whit Cooper
decd. Petition filed 4 Jany 1859, January 1858 court. Petition of Jesse C. Cooper as Trustee by contract between John T.
Postlewaite and Anna Eliza Cooper, John T. Postlewaite and Ann
Eliza Cooper , formerly Anna Eliza Cooper, Whitmel L. Cooper
and Jesse C. Cooper, as next friend of Jesse C. Cooper,Jr. who
has no guardian. Whitmel Cooper attained majority age 21 years
and another of them Anna Eliza has in the last few months in-
ter-married with John T. Postlewaite. Decree was issue Jany
1858 (Dockets 1885-1870. p.84.)

        John Anderson, carriage and wagon maker of Paris, was
born in Pennsylvania in 1825 son of Robert and Elizabeth Anderson. The father was a native of Penn. born about 1797 a stone
cutter and farmer. Mrs. Anderson was born in Penn. and died in
1882. John Anderson married in 1855 Isabella W. Brown born in
Penn. 1829. They were Cumberland Presbyterians.

SOME HENRY COUNTY MARRIAGES

* * * *

NOTE: These are by no means all the marriage records to be found in Henry County, in the courthouse. The early marriages are scattered through several books which contain other items as well as marriages: there is no index to the early marriages; in order to locate what one wishes it is necessary to read item by item and page by page of very very poor script. The first book available with marriages is badly in need of lamination and repair; The second book is also in bad condition but the script is somewhat better. There is no index to this book; The third book is without a good index. The marriages given herein have been copied with the consumption of much time. All the marriage records from 1830 seem to be in the courthouse but the condition or indexing or lack of indexing makes it a very slow project of research. ERW.

MARRIAGE BOOK No.1.

Jany 9th, 1838, Bloomfield Boden to Sarah Kimbrough. No return. (No. 6.p.1.)

March 14, 1838 James Freeman and Frances Alexander, Married 15 March 1838. (No. 38.p.1.)

February 7, 1838, William T. Haskell to Sarah J.P. Porter Married February 7, 1838. (No.15.p.1.)

July 14, 1838 Ezekiel Green Lafayette Bumpass to Julia Carson , Married July 15, 1838. (No.70 p.2)

November 3, 1838 Isaac Wimberly to Sarah Shankle. (No.126 p.3)

November 20, 1838 Marquis L. Glover to Obedence Allen. No return. (No. 31.p.3)

January 15, 1839 Wilson Shankle and Sarah Wimberly. Married January 17, 1839. (No. 4. p.3)

March 8, 1839 Henry A. Paschal and Wealthy Northington, Married March 9. (No. 30 p.4)

March 12, 1839, William Parker and Frances M.Courts, No return. (No.32 p.4.)

June 22,1839 Willie A. Morgan to Ann E Courts, June 23,1839 date solemnized. (No.53.p. 4)

September 4,1839 Blount Cooper and Elizabeth Freeman. Married Sept.5, 1839. (No.76 p.4)

October 29, 1839 Core Cooper and Elizabeth Thomas. Married on November 3,1839. (no. 101 p.5)

November 20, 1839 Green B. Dillahunty and Susan C. Wall. No return. (No. 107 p.5)

December 25, 1839 Newton A. Dinwiddie and Charlotte M. Dillahunty December 26, 1839. (No. 116 p.5)

January 23, 1840 William Markham and Lucinda J. Bumpass, 20 Jany 1840. (No.10 p.5)

February 13, 1840 Marcilius H.Risen (?) and Susan A. Freeman, Feb. 13, 1840. (No.20,p.6)

April 4, 1840, Benjamin Dunlap and Louisa Dunlap, married April 5, 1840. (No. 33. p.6)

April 20, 1841. Joseph Lamb to Martha Potts by Thomas Potts, M.G (No.35, p.8.)

July 21, 1841.John G. Lamb to Letha E. Glover. (No.52.p.8)

September 27, 1842, John Dillahunty and Catharine F. Bells. No return. (No. 91 p.11)

August 31, 1842, Thomas Stewart and Fanny S. Freeman. No return shown. (No.82.p.11)

September 1, 1842, Thomas M. Wilson and Zilphy Gullage. No return. (No.83. p.11)

December 26, 1840, William Gulledge and Sarah Lax. No return. (No. 132 p.12)

March 16, 1843 Francis M.Dillahunty to Susan E. Carter. No return (No. 29. p.12)

July 15, 1843 David Lamb and Ann Dunn. Married July 21, 1843. (No.58.p.13)

James Boden and Amanda Courts, August 24,1843. Married same day. (No.69. p. 13)

July 4, 1843 Horace T. Blanton and Martha A. Lamb. no return shown (No.55 p.13)

August 31, 1843 James Giles to Hannah W. Caldwell. (No.72. p.13)

February 5, 1844, Isaac D. Cardwell and Nancy E. Rogers. Married March 12. (No.26.p.14).

November 15, 1844 executed. E. Campbell and M.M. Cooper (No.103, p.17).

December 6, 1844. John Todd and Mary A.Bowden, Married on December 16, 1844. (No.110 p.17).

March 12, 1845, Preston Dunlap and Margaret Dunlap. Marriage day not shown. (No.41. p. 18).

May 16, 1846 Thomas D. Courts and Mary A. Paschall. Married on May 17, (No. 68 p.23).

July ___ 1846, George Freeman and Polly Poore. No return (No.79 p.24).

May 2, 1849 Azariah Smotherman and Mary R. Cooper, May 3, 1849. (No.62 p.35).

August 1, 1854 John Caldwell and Frances A. Blythe. No Return. (No. 68. p.67).

November 22, 1854 Wm.A. Trevathan and Sarah A. Kendall. November 23, 1854. (No.146 p.70).

December 5, 1854 James Lamb and Virginia Ray. (No. 150 p.70)

March 10, 1855 Saml P. Kendall and Elizabeth Easley. Married March 11, 1855. (No. 38 p.72).

March 28, 1855. John F. Kendall to Nancy Rumbley. March 29, 1855. (No.52. page 72).

August 27, 1855, J.J. Batson and Mary E. Lamb. (No.93.p.74)

November 12, 1855, J.H. Dunlap and M.J. Bell. Married November 13, 1855. (No.145 p.75).

October 11, 1856 N. J. Caldwell and R. E. Davis. Married October 8, 1856. (No.108p.81)

November 12, 1856 John H. McDonald and A.S. Caldwell. (No. 124.p.81)

October 29, 1857, William R. Cooper and Sarah Burnett. (No.118p.87).

December 23, 1857, David T. Bonner (Bomer ?) and Susan A Coldwell (Caldwell ?). (No.156 p.88).

March 13, 1858, Saml.T.McClean and Sarah J. Lamb. Married March 15, 1858. (No. 37 p.90).

March 31, 1858, James E. Freeman to Portia J. Allen. Married on April 7, 1858 (No.45. p.90).

June 2, 1858 , Jesse (P. or J. ?) Orr and Louisa Lamb. Does not show date returned. (No. 73 p.91).

June 16, 1858, Whitmel L.Cooper and Arkansas J. Kendall. No date solemnized shown. (No.76.p.91).

June 28, 1858, John W. Trevathan and Martha V. Caldwell. Married on June 29, 1858. (No.81 p.90).

July 19, 1858, Lazarus Williams and Mary J. Cooper. No date solemnized shown. (No.93.p.92).

Sept. 7, 1858. Walter B. Grizzard and Anna Courts, Presbyterian Church. Married 7 Sept. 1858. (No.104 p.92).

November 14, 1846, Jacob Foust and Mary Ann Dunlap. Married on the 15th November 1846. (No.132 p.26).

April 6, 1847 Miles P.Chandler and Helen Freeman. Date solemnized not shown. (No.35 p.28).

June 5, 1847, David S. Freeman to Mary E.Page. Married on June 10, 1847. (No.51 p.28).

July 15, 1847. William Kendall and Relley Ann Rumbley. Date it was solemnized not shown. (No.58 p.29).

August 17, 1847 Elisha Lamb to Elizabeth Jamison. They married on August 19, 1847. (No.67 p.29).

August 23 , 1847, Elijah Lamb to Nancy Lamb. Married on August 25, 1847 (No.73 p.29).

September 1, 1847 J.W.Cooper to Analiza Porter. They married Sept 2, 1847. (No.78 p.29).

February 26, 1848, James L. Freeman to Martha Nance. They married February 27, 1848. (No.38 p.32).

March 3, 1848, Samuel Linton to Reamy Bowden. Married March 1, 1848 (No.45 p.32).

January 26, 1849 , Wm.F.Cooper to Sarah Jane Jenkins. They married Jany 28, 1849 ,(No.15.p.39).

July 31, 1849, John Cooper and Martha Jane Phillips. Married on August 1, 1849. (No.91.p.40).

September 19, Frances M.Freeman and Amervea Cockrum. Married on Sept. 26, 1849. (No.111 p.41).

October 10, 1849. Edward F.Bumpass and Ethelander Wade.
(No.118 p.41).

November 29, 1849, David Kendall to Elizabeth J.Lee. No
date marriage was solemnized shown. (No.145 p.42).

June 18, 1851, James D. Porter, Jr. and Susan A.Dunlap at
the Cumberland Presbyterian Church. E.C. Trimble, Minister
of the Gospel. (No.18 p.50).

September 17, 1851. James I.Dunlap to Margaret I. Avin.
(No.87,p.51).

October 27, 1851, Washington Lamb to Hurett Flemming. Married
on the same day. (No.110 p.52).

July 21, 1852, W.H. Humphrey to Ann E.Freeman. (No.76 p.56)

August 9, 1852 , John C.P.Cooper to Verginia Allen. Married
August 10, 1852. (No.82 p. 56).

October 14, 1852 , Wm.H. Vandyche and Sarah J.Martin. No
return. (No.108 p.57).

February 2, 1853, James W.Willis to Mary A.Caldwell. Married
on February 3, 1853. (No. 17. p.59).

April 11, 1853 , W.D. Poyner to Amanda M.F. Bumpass. (No.
39 p.60).

April 23, 1853 ,Thomas Lamb and Sophronia Brogden. (No.
42 p.60).

April 26, 1853, Benj.F.Lamb and Henrietta Cooney executed
according to law.April, 26, 1853 . C.J.Bradley, minister.
(No.43.p.60).

May 4, 1853, J.N.M.Lynch to Margaret I.Kendall. (No.48.
p.60).

May 21, 1853, Thomas J.Kendall and Martha E.Caldwell. Married
May 22, 1853. (No.56 p.61).

January 31, 1854, James T. Cooney and Emma J.Bowles by
Edmond Almond J.P. (No.162 p.64. This must have been
issued January 7 and married January 31, but the dates are
reversed in the recording.).

January 11, 1854 , Martin D.Lamb and Virginia C.McClain.
Married 12 January 1854. (No. 7, p.65).

February 3, 1854. Benjamin Kendall to Martha A.Russell.
Married February 5, 1854. (No.21.p.65).

March 4, 1854, V.C.Travatheon and Eliza J.Kendall. Married on March 5, 1854. (No.34.p.66).

November 17, 1858, John A.Allen to Mary E.Kendall. (No.145.p. 94).

December 16, 1858, William Call and Mary Lamb. (No.166.p.94).

May 17,1859,E.R.Bumpass to Kate E.Willis. Married April 8, 1859 (No. 57.p.97).

December 12, 1859, James P. Lamb to Anna I.Wallie. (No.154, p.100).

April 12, 1860 , Benjamin H.Diggs to Sarah T or P? Freeman. (No.50 p.103).

MARRIAGE BOOK B. 1860-1877

December 14, 1863, F.P.Lamb to Clementine Sweat. Married on December 19, 1863. (No..112 p.13).

January 27, 1864, James P.Cooper and Martha Blantan. (No.8, p.14).

February ____ 1865, Robert Cooper and Elizabeth Pierce. Married February 5, 1865. (No.22 p.214)

January 12, 1865, J.P. Dunlap and Mary M. Parker. (No.27. p.214).

May 6, 1865, Green Boden and Virginia Tombs, No return. (No. 43 p.215). The same entered again as No.50. but no return.

May 29, 1865, G.F.Paterson to Sallie Boden. Married May 31, 1865. (No. 45.p. 215).

August 25, 1865, Henry Curle to Lizzie Vandyche, No return. (No. 81 p.217).

September 16, 1865, John Bowden and Mahala Porter, (No.82.p. 217).

September 22, 1860, Robert J.Caldwell and Rosannah S. Walker. Married September 26, 1860. (No.98. p.1).

November 15, 1860, James A.Cooper and Rebecca J.Turner. Married November 18, 1860. (No.126, p.2).

November 15, 1860 John M.Williams to Barbary A.Cooper. Married November 18,1860. (No.127 p.2).

December 24, 1860,Samuel H. Caldwell to Mary R.Thompson. (No. 160 p.3).

January 21, 1861, Louis C.Cooney to Clementine Baker. Married January 28, 1861 (No.19.p.4).

June 4, 1861 James M.Ray and Alace A.Coldwell. (No.51.p.5)

December 27, 1861 Silas Moore and Sophronia H.Lamb. Married on December 28, 1861. (No.100 p.6).

November 22, 1865, B.B.Lamb to Elizabeth J. Thompson. No return. (No.138.p.218).

January 3, 1866, I.Y. Freeman to Helen Bowden. Married on January 24, 1866. (No. 22 p 220).

MARRIAGES 1838-1860

April 2, 1838. Charles Spencer to Mary Lefever. Married April 2, 1838. (No.45).

June 7, 1838, Booker Cunningham and Amy Watkins. (No.61).

November 3, 1838. Isaac Wimberly and Sarah Shankle.Married November 8, 1838.   (No.126).

May 30, 1840. William Walker and Martha I.Smith, no return (No.45).

December 27, 1842, Henry W. Walker and Nancy Goode. Married on December 28, 1843. (No.133).

March 29, 1843. John Walker and Sally Rice. Married March 30, 1843. (No. 35).

November 15, 1847, Henry P.Wimberly and Lucinda P. Stroud. Married November 16, 1847. (No. 104).

March 20, 1847. David Walker and Mary Ann McCarty. Married March 20, 1847. (No. 45).

April 10, 1847, James Walker and Sarah Street. (No.55).

May 12, 1847. John Wimberly and Sue Frazier. (No.66).

William Walker and Lucy A.M.Whitfield. Married June 15, 1848 (No.84).

January 8, 1850, Wilson R.Walker and Nancy Weeks. no return (No.5).

January 19th, 1850. George W.Wimberly and Nancy Clayton. Married January 20th, 1850. (No.10).

February 23, 1850, James H.Walker and Lucy Page. (No.6).

March 15, 1850 Wm.P.Wimberly and Elizabeth Whitfield. Married March 17, 1850. (No.43).

August 13, 1850 Isham Walker and Rachell P.Hampton. (No.90).

November 9, 1850,Henry W.Walker and Mary E.Archie.(no.131).

April 19, 1851 Lewis Wimberly and Mary C.Roberts, April 20,1851 was the day solemnized. (No. 38).

May 12, 1851, Hugh R.Cunningham and Margaret C.Janes (or Jones?) Married on May 15, 1951. (No.49).

August 5, 1852, Wm.D.Wimberly and Milberry R.L.Lee. (No.80).

May 2, 1853, Noah Wimberly and Martha Lee. Married May 13, 1853. (No.46).

March 7, 1854, Miles C.Cunningham and Matilda J. Webster. Married March 9.1854 (No.39).

December 12, 1854, Vincent B.Walker and Louisa J.Kendall. (No. 153).

February 17, 1855. John H.Routon and Martha Wimbush, Married February 19, 1855 (No.30).

July 9, 1857. Eli Walker and Malinda Jane Steely. (No. 67).

June 31, 1858, Stephen P. Routon and Mary C.Haynes. (No.72).

July 21, 1858, Philip Q. Routen and Sarah A. Wimbush. July 22, 1858. (No.95).

November 7, 1859, Robert T.Walker and Ellen Archer. (No.__?)

July 24, 1860, Henry P.Wimberly and Hannah M. Roberts. (No.72).

August 4, 1860, William F.Walker, and Dorcas J. Cline. (No.76).

Miscalleneous Marriages

A. E.Cooper and Bettie Dinwiddie, December 15, 1877. (Book 1877-1881 p.54).

James M.Cooper and Miss Lucinda E. Lemonds. 7 August 1880 (Book 1877-71 p.431).

W.C.Cooper and Miss Hattie Givens, Nov. 27, 1880. (Book 1877-1881 p.471).

Jno.M.Cooper and Miss M.A.Thompson. December 11, 1880. (Book 1877-1881 p.477).

S.L.Cooper and Miss J.E.King. January 4, 1881 (Book 1877-81 p 503).

Ben. H.Freeman and Miss Mary H.Lamb. 12 May 1880. Signed Jno.R. Rison. (Book 1877-81 p.413).

G.C. Freeman and Miss E.C.Wade. December 1, 1881 (Book 1877-1881 p.472).

J.H(ouston) Lamb and Cecelia Humphreys, January 26,1880.
(Book 1877-1881 p.380).

Wm. Lamb and Miss Mollie Hudgens. January 20, 1881.(Book
1877-81 p.512).

W.L.Wiggins and Miss Salina Lafon, January 29,1879.(Book
1877-81 p.234).

James Monroe Klutts and Miss Caroline Francis Jarrett.
July 9, 1881 (Book 1877-81 p 561).

General Cooper and Adaline Simmons (in one place)
Adaline Williams (in another place). Sept.20,1876.
(Book 1872-77 p.490).

Alex. (X) Courts and Laura Kendall, February 19,1876.
Signed by Peter (X) Blakemore. (Page 437 Book 1872-77).

Barrum Lamb and Mahala Johnson. October 17,1872 (Book
1872-77 p.21).

Joseph Lamb and Ariminty P.Holley. April 30,1873 (Book
1872-77 p.101).

W.T.Lamb and Sarah J. Ross. December 23,1875. (Book 1872
-1877 p.403).

E. Lamb and Martha Walls, July 13,1876. (Book 1872-77
page 468).

Jno.L.Lamb and Margaret A Snyder, January 22,1877 (Book
1872-1877 p. 558)

Dick Vandyck and Ellen Jackson, 21 December 1872 (Book
1872-77 p.57).

W.A.Vandyck and Mattie A.Barber, December 21,1876, (Book
1872-77 p.539).

H.V.Freeman and Mrs. Bettie B (or T?) Freeman. December
31,1874 (Book 1872-77 p.310)

Isaac Freeman and Abby Pillow, April 19, 1877. (Book 1872-
77 p.586).

Randolph Dunlap and Edith Calhoune, October 2, 1872. (Book
1872-77 p.12).

John Dunlap and Wilmot Howard, May 7,1873 (Book 1872-77
p.104).

Thomas Dunlap and Sallie Bowles, Dec.28,1874 (Book 1872-77 p.307).

Richard W. Dunlap and Charlie Bell Lamb. October 28,1875. (Book 1872-77 p.374).

Thomas Dunlap and Lucy Randle, January 17,1876 (Book 1782-77 p.416).

F.T.Dunlap and Margaret Robenson, June 10,1876. (Book 1872-77 p.463).

Jack Dunlap and Laura Porter, 29 July 1876. (Book 1872-77.p. 470).

Columbia Dunlap and Harriet Covington, Feby 3, 1877 (Book 1872 -1877 p.564).

Frank Dunlap and Bell Jones, 22 Feby 1877. (Book 1872-77 p. 574)

Henry Dunlap and Phillips Duncan. Feb.9,1877. (Book 1872-77 p.577).

Miss Mary E. Vandyche and Crawford C. Chambers. March 26, 1921 (Book 1920-22, p.301).

Miss Goldie Dunlap and Tally (Sally ?) E.Alexander, March 5, 1921.

Dr.Milton Cayce Wiggins , M.D. and Miss Lucille De Nevers Lamb, November 10,1920. Signed by Lamberth Hancock and Leslie T. Bolton. M.D. (Book 1920-22 No.427.P.182).

Yewel Lamb and Miss Ruby Marine. Sept.17,1920. (Book 1920-22 p. 137)

Miss Mary Lamb and Earl Wyatt, October 19,1920. (Book 1920-22 p.162).

Earley Lamb and S.E. Mills. Sept.22, 1921 (Book 1920-22 p.395)

Miss Cordie May Lamb and J.O.Miles. Dec. 23, 1921. (Book 1920-1922 p.471).

Shirley Lamb and Miss Lillie McDongal. Jan. 21, 1922 (Book 1920 -22 p.504).

W.L.Lamb and Miss Daisey Williams, Feb.25, 1922 (Book 1920-22 p.527).

James Lamb and Miss Sallie Scruggs, 10 October 1882 (Book 1881-82 p.119).

James Lamb and Emily Jane Charlton. 4 December 1882 (Book 1881-82 p.143).

Lewis Lamb and Miss Nancy Charleston, January 17, 1883. (Book 1881-1886. p. 174)

William J.Lamb and Miss Nancy A.Bonner. October 22,1883. (Book 1881-86 p. 238).

William Lamb and Miss Mary E.Overcast. 27 October 1884. (BoOk 1881-86 p.365)

Wm.J.Lamb and Miss Laura Lamb. July 14, 1885 (Book 1881-86 p.450).

Arthur B.Lamb and Miss Minnie Leila Caldwell, Bond November 4, 1885, Signed Thomas P.White. (Book 1881-86 No.184, P.494).

Joseph G Lamb and Miss Ardelle Sanders. 26 November 1885 (Book 1881-86 p.503.)

George M.Cooper and Miss Ada Burron (Bunon ?), March 30, 1884 (Book 1881-86 p.314).

Wm.R.Cooper and Sarah A. Hudgens, 18 March 1885. (Book 1881-86 p.423).

James P. Cooper and Miss Ada Hill. February 7, 1882. (Book 1881-6 p.71).

C.E.Cooper and Miss Sarah A.Lacy. January 1, 1883 (Book 1881-86 p.165).

W.R.Dunlap and Miss E.E. Hudspeth. Sept. 6, 1884 (Book 1881-86, p. 345).

Robert R. Wiggins and Miss Alleen Howard, October 11, 1884. (Book 1881-6 p. 357).

Joseph C.Wiggins and Miss Belle Mathis. May 27, 1885 (Book 1881-6 p.441).

William Cooper and Elvira Brookes. Oct. 1, 1838 (Book 1838-60 p.3. No.116).

Feb.11, 1839 , Howell Olive and Ann Lions. (Book 1838-60 p.3.)

July 30, 1839, Ralph G.Alexander and Nancy Gwinn. (No.65 p. 4. Book 1838-60).

James M.Mathias and M.M. Alexander, March 23, 1839 (Book 1838-60 p ___ No.37).

June 22, 1839. Willie A.Morgan and Ann E.Courts, (Book 1838-60 .No.53).

October 16, 1838, Riley F.Nix and Mary A.Alexander, (Book 1838-60 p.3 No.115).

June 14, 1848, Isaac D.Gore and Sarah Alexander, (Book 1838-60 p. 2 No.63).

February 8, 1838, William R.McFarland and Amantha Dunlap (Book 1838-60 p.1.No.16).

November 5, 1839, Reubin M.Alexander and Nelly Hart. (Book 1838-60, p. 5 No.____).

Joseph M.Wade and Cintha A.Alexander. October 12, 1839 (Book 1838-60 p.5).

October 12, 1839, John Mathias and Sarah A.Alexander. (Book 1838-1860)

Samuel B.Hill and Sarah A.Alexander, November 21, 1839 (Book 1838-1860 p.5).

December 30, 1839, Thomas C.Mason and Elizabeth M.Williams (Book 1838-60 p.5).

January 21, 1840, Theophilus Ellis and Sarah Alexander, (Book 1838-60 p.5)

January 26, 1841, Ashley Olive and Caroline Berary (?), (Book 1838-60 p.7).

October 20, 1841, Samuel W.Mathias and Mary Ann Alexander (Book 1838-60 p.9).

October 24, 1841, James Warmack and Permelia Humphrey (Book 1838-1860 p.9).

April 7, 1842, William Williams and Bethsheda Marberry. (Book 1838-1860 p.10).

June 7, 1842, William Ellison and Caroline Beachamp (Book 1838-1860 p.10).

August 8, 1842 , Thomas C.Starks and Winney Umphres (Book 1838-1860 p.11).

September 1843, Wilson Kendall and Eliza Copeland. (Book 1838-60 p.12).

August 5, 1844, William Olive and Martha I. Norton (Book 1838-60 p.16).

October 29, 1844, James Kendall and S.C.Warren (Book 1838-60 p. 16).

E. Campbell and M.M.Cooper, No date. (Book 1838-60 p.17)

May 15, 1845, Jacob Latimer and Margaret E.Dunlap. (Book 1838-60 p.19).

Moses D.Francis and Harriett Chandler,August 9, 1845, (Book 1838-60 p.19).

March 4, 1846, John M. Alexander and Elizabeth M. Acuff, (Book 1838-60) p.23).

March 19, 1846, Jefferson Alexander and Eliza Alexander. (Book 1838-60) p.23).

September 16, 1846, Hamilton Alexander and Martha J.Mathis. (Book 1838-60 p.25).

Sept. 11, 1846 William Alexander and Aditha Stephens. (Book 1838-60 p.25).

February 25, 1847 Simpson Alexander and Martha S.Haynes, (Book 1838-60 p 27).

November 18, 1847, Wm.S.Shell and Eliza Alexander. (Book 1838 -1860 p. 27).

April 1, 1847, Daner P.Alexander and Mary Ann E.Powell.(Book 1838-60 p.28).

April 6, 1847 Miles P. Chandler and Helen Freeman (Book 1838- 60, p.28).

April 18,1847, Henry S. Oliver and Mary Ann Malier (Book 1838- 60 p.28).

April 19, 1847, Moses A Duner and Oneda C.Alexander (Book 1838-60 p. 28).

February 19, 1848, John P.Alexander and Emily Stephens,(Book 1838-60 p.32).

J.O.Alexander and Mary Jane Jones, February 29,1848 (Book 1838-60 p.32).

March 1, 1849, Samuel W. Alexander and Edy C.Smotherman, (Book 1838-60 p.34).

September 27, 1848, John M.Alexander and Lydia McLeer (?), (Book 1838-60 p 37).

November 4, 1848, H.Humphrey and Sarah Ann Coats , (Book 1838-60 p.38).

December 5, 1848, M.D.Stephenson and Rebeccah Olive, (Book 1838-60 p.38).

November 14, 1848, Elias Tomlinson and Flora M.Alexander, (Book 1838-60 p.38).

October 23, 1848, Thomas McClain and Ann Humphrey, (Book 1838-60 p.38).

September 21, 1849, Franklin Ray and Susan I.Nix, (Book 1838-60 p.40).

November 10, 1849, Abner C.McGehee and Susan Chandler (Book 1838-60 p.40)

January 2, 1850, Berry P.Alexander and Mary Jane Alexander (Book 1838-60 p.43)

W.H.R. Alexander and Lucretia Butler (Book 1838-60 p.43) Date being February 28,1850.

March 12, 1850, John W. Watkins and Martha Jane Oliver. (Book 1838-60 p.44)

April 14, 1850, Charles Myck (Myrich ?) and Sarah Alexander (Book 1838-60 p.44).

June 20, 1850, Oliver C. Wagner and Joy Catherine Olive, (Book 1838-60 p 45).

August 11 , 1850 Willis G.Williams and Esther C.Pettyjohn.(Book 1838-60 p.46)

September 3, 1850, John W.Dunlap and Malinda L.Parker. (Book 1838-60 p.46).

September 13, 1850, Thomas R.Milam and Lugonia Janes (Book 1838-60 p.46)

September 11, 1850, John Jayen and Phebe Olive, (Book 1838-60 p.46).

November 14, 1850, George D.Odance (?) and Margarett L.Anderson (Book 1838-60 p.47)

_____29, 1851, Richard H.Jones and Jane Humphrey (Book 1838-60 p.51).

_____ 1851 (gone) Thomas Jenkins and   (Blank) (Book 1838-60 p.51).

February 18, 1852. S.W.Alexander and Elizabeth Stiles. (Book 1838-60 p.54).

Archibald Philips and Mary Olive, March 5, 1852 (Book 1838-60 p.54)

January 22, 1852, Tazewell M. Jones (or Janes ?) and Winney Humphreys (Book 1838-60 p.54).

June 17, 1852, James F.Alexander and Elizabeth Jobe. (Book 1838-60 p.55).

July 1, 1852, Peter Lacewell and B.A. Alexander, (Book 1838-60 p.55).

July 21, 1852, W.H.Humphrey and Ann E.Freeman (Book 1838-60 p.56).

December 11, 1853, F.E. Alexander and Lovely A.Bratton.(Book 1838-60 p.58).

December 13, 1852, J.B.Milam and E.J. Allen (Book 1838-60 p.58).

December 23, 1852, B.T.Howard and Emeline E.Kendall. (Book 1838-60 p.58).

January 8, 1853, Asa Humphrey and Elizabeth C.Coats.(Book 1838-60 p.59)

April 26, 1853, Benj.F.Lamb and Henrietta Cooney,(Book 1838-1860 p.60.)

May 4, 1853, J.N.M.Lynch and Margaret J.Kendall, (Book 1838-60 p.60).

October 1, 1853, James Stem and Edith A.Kendall.(Book 1838-60 p.62).

N.L.Lewis and M.A. Cooper, October 11, 1853 (Book 1838-60 p.62.)

January 21, 1854, Henry P.Stephens and Nancy M.Chandler. (Book 1838-60 p.65).

October 13, 1854, Ira Humphreys and Mary Ann Mathis. (Book 1838 1860 p 69).

October 22, 1853. Wm.A. Travatham and Sarah A.Kendall.(Book 1838-60 p 70).

January 9, 1855, James M.Olive and Mary A.Moody (Book 1838-60 p.71).

August 21, 1855, Robert Lowry and Elizabeth Alexander (Book 1838-60 p.73)

November 15, 1855, Mandethea Alexander and Nancy Gholston (Book 1838-60 p.76).

January 2, 1856, Green Manly and Lucretia Alexander (Book 1838-60 p.77).

May 1, 1856, J.D.Alexander and Louisa A.Goodall (Book 1838-60 p.79).

September 29, 1856, Wm.A.Anderson and Caroline H.Smyth (Book 1838-60 p.80).

January 29, 1857. W.G.Randle and Sarah E.Kendall. (Book 1838-60 p.83).

July 3, 1857, Benjamin Kendall and Geraldine R.Russel.(Book 1838-60 p.85).

October 16 (?), 1857, William R.Cooper and Sarah A.Burnett (Book 1838-60 p.87).

January 12, 1858, John A. Bachnuner (?) and Mary E.Humphreys. Book 1838-60 p.89)

January 19, 1858, John B. Hutchins and Angalen R.Alexander (Book 1838-60 p.89).

> Note: A few of the marriage records I observe been given twice. In these instances they are found recorded twice.   ERW

==

INFORMATION

The records in the Clerk & Master's Office at Paris, the County Seat of Henry County, Tennessee, are a gold mine of history and genealogy, but they are difficult to work in as there is no master index or name index as the case may be. The docket book only shows the style of the case and the year, but the transcripts and the records in the books which are recorded as well as those which are filed without being recorded in books, are most detailed and valuable. There should be some way to preserve these original papers.

In the Clerk of the County's office there are to be found a number of original wills which are not recorded in the record books or the will books. They are in files in the vault. These original papers hold many stories of the lives of the pioneer of Henry County. They are in most cases very fragile and should be preserved before they are lost completely.

The records in the deed books in the Register's office are in excellent condition for the most part. I do not think I have found any deed books missing in this office.

DEED, CUNNINGHAM TO SUTTLE

* * *

I, Sarah Ann Cunningham widow and relick of John Cunningham, Deceased, have this day Sold and do hereby transfer and convey to E.J. Suttle and his heirs forever for the consideration of Seventy five Dollars to me in hand paid all my right of dower in the real estate of said John Cunningham decd, lying in the State of Tennessee, Henry County, and District 14, containing by survey forty acres more or less and bounded as follows Viz - Beginning at Wm. Colmres (?) N E corner thence west 90 poles to a small white oak with hickory and Black oak pointers, thence north 27 poles to a white oak thence west 60 poles, thence north 11 poles to Suttles corner, thence East 54 poles to a stake with red oak pointers. Suttles S east corner thence north 27 to a stake thence east 96 poles to a black oak Black and post oak pointer thence south 65 poles to the beginning to have and to hold the same to the said E.J. Suttle his heirs and assigns forever, I do covenant with the said E.J. Suttle that I am lawfully Seized of said land have a good right to convey it and that the same is unincumbered I do further covenant and bind myself my heirs that I will warrant and forever defend the title of said dower to the said E.J. Suttle his heirs and assigns among the time of my natural life and no longer. Given under my hand and seal this 30th day of May 1853. Signed Sarah Ann Cunningham (Seal) Test; S.A. Brizendine. P.D. Walker. State of Tennessee Henry County. Personally appeared before me James McKay, clerk of the County Court for said County, Sarah Ann Cunningham the granter to the foregoing deed and acknowledged the same to be her act and deed on the day it bears date and for the purposes therein contained.
Witness my hand at office this 4th day of November 1856.---
James McKay, clerk. By B.B. Bunch, Deputy clerk.
(Deeds M. page 398.).

The articles and amount of sale of the estate of Hugh Cunningham decd. (long record covered more than two pages). The widow is shown as Lucinda Cunningham. Among those who made purchases at the sale: William Howard, James Walker, Russell Cunningham, Robert Poyner, John Hartgrove, Gilbert Ary, Wm.Stiles, Miles Cunningham, L.M.Tharpe (Thorpe), Luce M.Thorpe, James Walker, Milly Cunningham and others, 5 Jany 1857 (Deed Book I (1856-63,p.73 etc).

Property of D.C. Cunningham, decd. covers three pages. Among the purchasers: H.R.Cunningham, Wm.Futrell, Wm.Baugh R.D. Coldwell, James Thralkill, James Hays (?), B.F.Parrish, Robert Duger, William Edmunds, Thomas Carroll, Jerry Dugger, H.F.Milton (Melton), Sol.Fuller, P.M.Miller, M.C.Cunningham, G.W. Hendrix. Dated 31 March 1858. (Book I,1856-63,p.201)

WALKER RECORDS

* * *

William S.Walker Power of Attorney by John J.Walker.

Know all men by these presents that I John J. Walker of the County of Warren and State of Tennessee in the year of our Lord 1837 on the fifteenth day of November having for divers good causes thereunto moving me made and constitute my Son William S.Walker to be my lawful attorney to act for me in and in my name and behalf and in the name and behoof of his mother Elizabeth Walker in all matters relating to the division and distribution of a part of the Estate of James Harper decd and he is hereby authorized to act for me in the said Estate and use all such means for the dividing and recovering a part of said Estate as is coming to us as a legatee of said Harper decd as we could do if we were there personally present also to give any receipt or acquittance at his discretion that might be wanted for the completion of said business in as ample a manner as I could do were I there present. Signed sealed and c. the day and year first above written. John J.Walker (Seal). Elizabeth R. Walker (Seal). Attest, John Cain, Wm.White, Proved in Warren County, Tennessee November 17, 1837. Recorded in Henry County, Tennessee Deeds F page 150.

Whereas William D.Walker, Lafayette Rose and Tabitha Rose his wife formerly Tabitha Walker, have a fee simple interest of 2/s in the Remainder to take effect and be united with the possession after the death of Ann Walker who has a life Estate in the same , A tract of land in Henry County, District No.1. estimated 54 acres. etc. 23 Dec. 1853 . Signed: V.L.Rose,W.D.Walker Tabitha Rose (formerly Walker). (Deeds K p.543).

F.C.Gray and F.L. Manley and Vincent B.Walker of Henry County, 114 acres land in the name of Walker & Manley, land granted by State of Tennessee to Nathaniel Williams heirs 200 acres Grant No. 577. Range 6 Section 8. Signed F.C. Gray , 25 Feby 1853.(Deed. K.p.497).

In the original unrecorded wills on file in Henry County, is that of James Walker, Noncupative will. Departed this life March 20,1856. Refers to children and wife. Son Richmond. He wanted to be buried at the graveyard where William Whitfield and his wife are buried. The will was written down by Jno.H. Williams. March 26, 1856. It was witnessed by D.M.L.Walker and J.R.Walker.

A.J.Walker's will on file in un-recorded wills in Henry County, calls for nephew W.E.Hopkins, 2 nieces Hanner and L.A. Shankle 26½ acres land. Refers to Sister S.M.Shankle. Niece, L.A.Shankle. Sister Hanner Wimberly's five children. Appoints G.W.Hopkins and Hannah A.Shankle executors. 23 August 1890. Signed A.J(X) Walker, exec. Witnesses, Jas. A. Williams. W.D. Wimberly.

William Walker's will; names wife Gillie Walker, as executor. Dated June 9, 1897.

D.M.L. Walker's will August 10, 1880 (un-recorded and found in file in Courthouse), Calls for brother A.J. Walker. Sister L.M. Shankle. refers to three nieces.

According to the 1850 census of Henry County, Elizabeth Walker, was born in Virginia and was at that time 72 years of age. She lived in the 13th Civil District of the county, and was a neighbor of Daniel Avery and wife who came from North Carolina. Avery was seventy years of age and his wife Rebecca was fifty according to the census report. Both families had children.

===

Dots and Dashes

In Chancery Court, March 18, 1867, a suit John M. Rumbly et als VS. John S.Easley et als. Original Bill. Devereaux J.Kendall was appointed Trustee for Belinda H. Easley, wife of Defendant John S. Easley, and Rilly Ann Kendall wife of Defendant William Kendall. Belinda H. and Rilly Ann were due from the executors of Thomas Rumbley, decd. Ordered John M.Rumbley pay over to the Kendall,etc.

The 1867 docket of the Chancery Court of Henry County, appears filled with cases in which the Kendalls, the Edmunds, the Cooneys, were involved. They do provide much valuable information of a genealogical nature.

SOME PROMINENT CITIZENS IN THE CIVIL DISTRICTS.

* * * * *

Space will not permit giving a complete list and detail sketch of each prominent family or citizen in the various Civil Districts of Henry County, after the county was divided into Civil Districts, but the following will aid the student to more or less the location in the county of some of the most outstanding families and the families with whom they intermarried.

The First Civil District included the town of Paris.

Dr. Sidney B.Aden, from South Carolina, born about 1810 was well established in the county by 1850. Dr. E.T.Taliaferro from Virginia, a young physician was already engaged in his profession in Paris, where he and his family had located.

Colin D.Venable, a Kentuckian, age 35 years , was clerk of the County Court in 1850, and resided in Paris.

E.F.Bumpass was the Innkeeper in 1860. He was born in South Carolina about the year 1801-2. James T.Cooney, a young and prominent man of only eighteen years of age , a native of the county, was living at the Inn.

M.C. Bowles, a Virginian, who had lived some time in Kentucky before settling in Henry County, was a merchant and was one of the wealthiest in the town in 1850. He was born about 1805/6. His wife was Angeline and born about 1811. Their children living in their home in the year of 1850 when the census was taken were: Mary Eliza age 18, Ellen age 17, Inugenia P. age 15, Angeline T. age 13, William M. age 11, John James age 9, Sarah age 7, Joshua B, age 5, Joseph T age 3, and Alben S. age 2 months , were all born in Kentucky. Since the youngest child was given as born in Kentucky and only two months old, it would indicate that the family had only recently settled in Paris.

Hiram F.Cummins who was the editor of the "Paris Sentinel" newspaper, is shown in the 1850 census enumerated as having been born in Kentucky and was then 31 years of age. His wife Eliza Jane was 28 years of age and was a native of Missouri. Their children Emma J. age 4, Alice age 2 and an infant not then named age 3 months, were all born in Tennessee.

Hezekiah Callender was a young man of twenty-eight or or about years of age with a family. He was the town "Tailor". Living in his household other than his immediate family were: Cynthia Blythe age 60 born in North Carolina. Also Thinea Blythe (a female) age 17 and A.G.Blythe (a male) age 15 both born in Tennessee.

Judge William F.Fitzgerald, a native of Maryland, age 51 in 1850 was one of the wealthiest men in Paris at that time.

John H.Dunlap, age 48, a lawyer, with a family including Marislla age 35, born in Kentucky, Susan E age 18, William 16, Bethay Ann 13, John age 10, and Hugh age 6, all born in Tennessee. In this family also lived Polly Beauchamp age 65 a native of Virginia.

James T.Dunlap also a Lawyer, age 37, in 1850, with his family, Jane B, age 27; Wm.C.,age 10; Susan G. age 8; Sarah Ann, age 7; James T, Jr., age 5; Ellen J. age 4; and Ripley C. age one month, all born in Tennessee.

The best established merchant in the town of Paris was probably Howell Edmunds in 1850. He was recorded as being worth $5000 in that yeat, indicating that he was a well-t-do man for his time. At that time (1850) his age was given as 58 years and his birth place as Virginia. His family included Martha age 18 years born in North Carolina, and Susan age 3 and Howel N. age four months the last two born in Tennessee.

Another lawyer in Paris in 1850 was Isaac B. Williams. He was then only about thirty five years of age. His wife was named Adeline H and was twenty-seven years old.Their children Fitzgerald age 8, Arabella age 4, and Frank were born in Tennessee and very likely in Paris.

Civil District No.2. of Henry County, was the home of John B.Edmiston, a North Carolinian, age 32 in 1850, whose profession was that of a lawyer. He had a young family at the time.

The Reverend W.L.James, a Virginian, age only 36 years in 1850, a Methodist Preacher, resided in this district. His wife was Mary age 35, a native of Tennessee. Their two children Eliza age 7 and George age 4 were born in Mississippi, but their youngest child William R. age one year was born in Tennessee; Thus it would appear that Rev.Mr.James had not long been in this section of the country.

Augustine Pearce from Virginia, a farmer, lived in this district in 1850. He was born about 1798/9. His wife seems to have been deceased by the time this census was taken.In his family lived Catherine age 22, pinkney age 20, and G.W. age 18, all three born in North Carolina. Mary age 12, Martha age 10, and Sally age 6 were born in Tennessee. The indication is strong this family lived in North Carolina and did not come to Tennessee until after 1832.

Anderson Chandler came from South Carolina to Tennessee. There was an Anderson Chandler who married in 1811 in Person County,North Carolina, but it does not seem these are the same men. Anderson Chandler who came

to Henry County, Tennessee was born about 1789. His wife was
named Ann and was a native of Tennessee.

        James B.Cooper lived in this district of the county.
He came from North Carolina where he was born about 1790. In
1850 his age was recorded as 60 years. His wife was Isabella
born about 1799 (age 51 in 1850). They had a large family
when they came to Henry County. Frances age 34, Nancy age 32,
Eliza age 30, and James J., age 23, as shown by the enumerat-
ion were all born in North Carolina. Martha age 20, William
age 18, Willis age 14, Joseph age 11 were born after the family
located in Tennessee.

        In Civil District No.3. Dr. James B.McClelland made
his residence. He was a native of North Carolina. By 1850 he was
established in practice of his profession, although only thirty-
four years of age. He was married and had a family.

        William H.Edmunds and family, and the family of
Preston Edmunds also resided in this district in 1850.

        In the Fifth Civil District, we find in 1850, William
Alexander who had come from South Carolina and settled. He was
born about 1790 and was a man of consequence. He probably resided
in Kentucky a few years before settling in Henry County. In 1850
in his household we find in addition to himself.--- W.W. Alexander age 26 born in South Carolina. Susan age 21, Catharine age 7,
Fanny age 4 and William age 2 years.The last four.born in
Kentucky. Catharine, Fanny and William were probably grandchildren of Mr. Alexander, and the children of W.W. and Susan
Alexander.

        In this district also lived Martin Freeman a prominent
citizen. In 1850 he was 57 years of age, born in North Carolina.
Dorothy no doubt his wife,was forty-seven years of age born in
Virginia. Their children living at home at the time were Hatfield
age 17, Martin Jr. age 14, and Lee age 12, all three born in
Tennessee.

        James H.Shaw a young Tennessean, only 24 years of age
was in the Cotton Manufacturing business in 1850. His wife Sarah
Jane was 20 years old and they had only one child Parella Newton
Shaw.

        The Pearce family and the Sixth Civil District of
Henry County, went together. By 1850 they were well rooted. John
Pearce a native of Virginia born about 1791/2 who married Margaret
_____?_____ born 1796 in North Carolina, and who had probably
remained in Virginia only a few years after his marriage but
who certainly lived in North Carolina for a time, migrated and
made a settlement in Henry County. The census of 1850 shows
John and Margaret Pearce had two children, Reuben age 22 and
Noah age 18, born in North Carolina, living.in what can well be

called the Pearce Settlemant. Next door to them lived
Wm. Bedford Pearce age 31 born Virginia, with Martha age
31 born N.C., and James M.age 4 and Elizabeth age 2 born
in Tennessee. Their neighbor was John Worrell Pearce
age 28 a native of Virginia with wife Margaret age 28,
William 4, Nancy 2, all born in Tennessee. Next door
to them lived Robert Pearce age 25 a native of North
Carolina with Mary age 21, born in Alabama, Thomas age 3
born in Tennessee. Not far away was Stephen Pearce age
21 also a native of North Carolina with Sally age 30 and
John six months of age. In the same community we find
John J.Pearce age 26, a native of Tennessee with Martha
age 23, W.A. age 2 and Dory Miller age 9, born in Tenn.

From this it seems that the Pearce family and
connections comprised a goodly portion of the district.

William Williams, a wagon maker from North Carolina
lived in the Seventh District of Henry County in 1850. He
was then 50 years old and in his family Elizabeth age 38
born in South Carolina. The family consisted of William
Ramsey age 18, Susan 16, Martha 14, Henry P. 12, Luthe
10, Howard (?) 8, Americus 6, Lewis A. P. 2, all born in
Tennessee.

Mr. Williams was probably the father of Thomas B.
Williams, age 21, who lived next door and whose wife
was Loving age 20. Thomas B.Williams was a wagon maker.

The relationship of the above family and that of
Henry L.Williams born about 1805 in North Carolina is not
presently known. Henry L. Williams household consisted of
Elizabeth age 52, Gabriel age 13, Edmund age 8, E.Jane
age 6, all born in Tennessee. Also, in this home lived
Charles Barnes age 17, Rebecca Barnes age 13, Edmund
Barnes age 15, Thomas R.Riley age 9, Albert I (J?) Williams
age 19 and Susan Williams age 16, natives of Tennessee.
(1850 Census).

Gideon French, a native of Georgia aged about 69
in 1850 with wife Rebecca age 61 born in Kentucky, were
residents of this district. In the same community nearby
resided Susannah French age 55 born in South Carolina, who
appears to have been a widow with a family of Wm.J.age 23,
A.J. age 18, Kezziah age 16 and Mary age 14 all born in
Tennessee. The relationship of these two families is not
at present known.

This was the community in which Dr. James D.Porter
made his home. Dr. Porter was a native of Kentucky and was
40 years of age in 1850. In his home resided Mary Cordelia
Porter age 16, Robert Porter age 11, and William Porter
age 7 years. The youngest in the family being Rebecca age 2.
Allen Justice age 35 a native of Tennessee and a Cumberland
Presbyterian minister resided in the home of Dr. Porter.

Another physician of that locality and district was
Dr. John W.Cooper age 32 born in North Carolina. He resided
next door to Dr. Porter. His family included Ann Eliza age 19,
Anna Medora age 1 and Ann Eliza age 11. (1850 census for ages)

L.D.Chauncey, a Blacksmith age 33 a native of New York
State resided next door to Dr. Cooper in the home of Jesse C.
Cooper who was himself age ·36 and a native of North Carolina.
Mr. Cooper was a farmer. His wife was Mary age 28 born in Kentucky.
In their family James age 8, Thomas age four months and
Whitmell age 14 years. (1850 census)

A young physician by the name of Robert A. Williams,
who in 1850 was only twenty-five years old and unmarried, lived
in the same neighborhood.

The most prominent family in the Eighth Civil District
of the county in 1850 was likely the Akers. They had been there
long enough to be well settled. The oldest living member of the
Akers settlement in 1850 appears to have been Lucinda Akers
age 60 a native of Kentucky. She was the head of household and
living with her Thomas age 36, Mary age 30, Frances Jane age 10,
Margaret Bell age 8, Julianna age 6, Robert F age 3, Thos. Z. age
10 months all born in Tennessee. Lucinda was probably the mother
of Thomas whose wife was Mary and the younger ones mentioned
were the children of Thomas and Mary. This is conjecture however.

Next door was the home of Isaac Akers age 28 born in
Alabama, a bricklayer, whose family appears as Sarah age 28
born in North Carolina, Thomas Wilson Akers age 3 and Mary Frances
Akers age one year born in Tennessee.

On the other side of Mrs. Lucinda Akers, and a near
neighbor, I find enumerated in 1850 Uriah Akers age 26 born in
Alabama. In his household Mary Wilson Akers age 22. Harris age
2 and Aden age 3 months.

This civil district was also the home of the Noels
who were from Virginia to Trigg County, Kentucky and later into
Henry County, Tennessee. Some of them moved into Davidson County,
Tennessee, where the family has long been of great prominence.
The Fousts, the Wrenns, and some of the Dunlaps lived in this
same community.

Possibly the oldest resident of the Nineth Civil District
was Joel Hicks, who in 1850 was 76 years of age. His wife Priscila
gave her age as 62 in 1850. At that time living with them was
Cassandra age 40, Silas age 26 and Louisa age 24 all natives of
North Carolina.

The Allen Bowles family came from Georgia to this
location before the 1850 census. With them in their home lived
Hiram W.Sullivan a school teacher. He probably married Frances
Bowles.

This was the same district in which the Dillahuntys, the Dinwiddies, some of the Dunlaps and some of the Alexanders located and made their homes.

In 1850 in the Tenth Civil District Gideon Milam from North Carolina age 52 and wife Nancy age 48 made their home. With them lived Jno.T. age 28, and, Cullen B. age 21 born born in Tennessee. In this family resided Sarah A. Bohannan age 14 years.

James W.Milam age 31, Mary Ann age 25, John G age 9, Thomas O. age 7, Samuel C, age 5, Wm.L. age 3. and Sarah Ann age 2 lived at the same place and community.

Bird Milam age 35 born in Virginia with Rouch age 33 Milly age 18, Joseph 12, Thomas 8, Richard 6, Nancy 4, and Aramanda age 1 year, all born in Tennessee, made their home.

George N.Foster from Virginia born about 1793/4 a millright with his family were in this district by 1850. Living in this household Lucy 44, William 19, Lafayette 17, Albun 15, Ann 14, Elizar 12, Martha 10, George 8, James 5, and Mary 3, all born in Tennessee.

John Grenada, a descendant of the same family in North Carolina as the famous pioneer minister John A. Granada, made his home.

Dr. W.H. Alexander from South Carolina, and some of the Coopers lived in this district also.

The Howards lived in the eleventh Civil District of the county in 1850. James H.Howard a substantial farmer came from North Carolina as did his wife Jackey. In 1850 he was 57 years of age and she was 49. Their family consisted of Angline age 24, Broadie age 18, Clementine age 16, DeWitt age 14, James G. age 12, Nathaniel age 9, and living with them was Celia Bowden age 82 born in Virginia. She was very likely the mother-in-law of Mr. Howard.

Just a few doors away lived Mennican Howard age 28, and family. His wife was Angeline age 26. In 1850 they had three children, Susanna age 7, Porter age 4 and W.A. age 2.

Another family well represented in this district was the Humphreys (Humphries, Umphres. etc). They also came from North Carolina. Henry, Thomas and Abner Humphreys were farmers and had large families.

In 1870 the Postoffice of the eleventh District of Henry County was New Boston. J.P.Bullock was the assistant Marshall in making the Federal Census of that year. Terrence Cooney had been the assistant Marshall or census taker in 1850. Mr. Cooney did not live in the disttict however.

Arthur Freeman gave his age as 50 years and born in Virginia, in 1850 to the census enumerator. His family consisted of Elizabeth age 30 born S.C., Ann age 18, Warren 16, William 14, Sarah 12 and Rebecca all born in Tennessee.

John C. Freeman and family also had settled in this community.

Elizabeth Cooper age 60 born in Virginia was living in the home of Ann Crutchfield and family in this district in 1850.

Benjamin Bowden from North Carolina age 47, and wife Emily age 41 from Kentucky with their family lived in this vicinity and district. Ivañ L. Alexander from South Carolina was also established in the district.

John Olive age 58 from North Carolina and family Mary 26, John H. 24, Mary 22, all born in North Carolina and Leroy age 18, and Leonidas age 18 born in Tennessee, were settled here. Next to them Josey Olive age 37 born in North Carolina with Jane H. Almarinda 12, Frances 11, James 8, Wiley 6, and Martha 4 all born in Tennessee.

A short distance away but still in this district resided Leroy Olive age 38 a native of North Carolina with a family - Harriett age 22 born N.C.; Cornelia age 14, Jefferson age 11, Louisa age 10, Rufus age 8, Parellee age 6, Milton age 4, and Elizabeth age 2 all born in Tennessee. In the home with them was Matthew Coley age 24 a native of North Carolina.

The Olive and the Alexander families intermarried. They had relatives just over the line in Kentucky, also.

Irvin B. Milam a merchant and Matthew Bowden, also a merchant made their homes in this section. Dempsey Bowden is also enumerated in 1850 in this section.

Terrence Cooney who kept the store and transacted a vast business at the Mouth of Sandy for many years, was the Assistant Marshall for the 11th, 12th, 13th, 14th, 15th and 16th Districts in 1850. He resided in the 15th District in 1850.

The Freemans, the Alexanders, the Williams were the most prominent families of the twelfth District in 1850.

When we come to the thirteenth Civil District of the County, we are in the home community of the Martin family. Abraham Martin born in North Carolina about 1807/8 seems to have been the main one of them. His wife was named Mary D and was born in Tennessee 1806/7. Their family consisted of several children.

The Martin's were neighbors to the family of K. D.

Hudgins and wife Sarah. Mr. Hudgins was a native of North Carolina, born about 1792, while his wife was about fourteen years younger.

James Hendricks, a Blacksmith, was in this district and was a native of this state born about 1805.

Moses Short, a North Carolinian born about 1782 made his home here. His wife Jemima was born about 1787. Mr.Short was a substantial farmer. He had lived in Kentucky before moving to Henry County, Tennessee. His daughter Rachel was born in Kentucky about 1816 and their son Fleming Short born around 1830 was a native of Kentucky.

Hugh M.Alexander and his wife Mary, came to Henry County, from Kentucky, where they were born , in about 1795 and she in 1801.They arrived in Henry County about 1829. Their son Meredith age 19, son John age ___ and daughter Eveline age 20 were all born after the parents moved to Tennessee. (1850 census)

Another Kentuckian who lived in this district in 1850 was Allen Dunlap, born about 1799 and his wife Ann born about 1802.

The Humphreys were also found in this district.

The John M.Alexander family from Virginia lived in this vicinity in 1850. His wife Lydia seems to have been a South Carolinian. He was 60 years old and she was 53 in 1850 according to the census. At that time in the household we find Jane 23, Martin Jones 10, both born in Kentucky; and, John C. 8, Thomas 6, both born in Tennessee. Susanna McClure three years old was living with this family.

James Paschal and wife Rachel were in this neighborhood. They were from North Carolina He was born about 1776 and his wife about 1786.

William Edmunds , the miller, and John Edmunds lived in this district, in 1850.

In the Fourteenth Civil District lived some of the Edmunds, the Browns, the Conyers, the Butterworths, the Hendricks, The Hunts and the Arbuckles.

The oldest person in this district in 1850 was possibly Elizabeth Martin born in Virginia about 1764 and living with Sarah Edmunds, who was born about 1800-1 in Virginia, who was the dead of the house.

Nearby Mrs. Edmunds, lived the family of Lewis Brown who, in 1850, gave his age as 75 born in North Carolina. In his family in that year were Martha Brown age 65 and Harrell Born age 27 born in North Carolina.

A short distance from the Browns lived Mordecai Conyers. He was born in North Carolina about 1781. His wife Elia-
abeth, born the same year as her husband, but was a native of
Kentucky. If they had children they were all married and away
from home in 1850.

Joseph Butterworth and wife Elizabeth came from
Virginia and located in this district where they reared their
family. Mr. Butterworth was seventy years of age and his wife
sixty-eight in 1850. The Butterworths were established in the
community long before 1840.

The Hendricks probably came from South Carolina. Martha
Hendricks was aged 85 years in 1850 and was residing in the home
of Daniel Hendricks whose wife was named Elizabeth. The Hendricks
came to Tennessee before Henry County was created for Daniel is
shown as being 45 years old born in Tennessee in the census.
Elizabeth, his wife was 36 and also a native of this state. Their
children William 16, Littleberry L. 14, James 12, Mirah M. 10,
Samuel 8, Goover C. 6, and Jane 7, were all born in Tennessee.
Also living in their home in 1850 was Phoebe Hunt age 30 years.

In the fifteenth District the most prominent and earliest families to settle were the Williams, the Arnolds, the
Olivers, and the Tiptons, this last family has been mentioned
earlier in our history.

William M.Williams, a substantial farmer and his
wife Nancy , had a family of small children in 1850. Living with
them was Martha Olive age 17 a native of Tennessee.

John H.Williams ,Jr., age 25, a native of Mississippi
was residing here also. His wife Elizabeth age 22 was also born
in Mississippi, and they had a family of young children. Living
with them was Nancy Olive.

James Arnold and wife Jane were from North Carolina.
in 1850 they had a family of minor children.

Frequently the name Oliver and Olive are confused. It
seems quite likely that both families were represented in Henry
County some time before 1850. A detailed study of these two names
may prove that they descend from a common ancestor: however,
what I have at this time clearly definites one as Olive and the
other as Oliver. The two above mentioned Nancy and Martha are
definitely shown as Olive. Living in the same community and
district we find Olivers.There were several families of them in
1850, residing close.together. Charity Oliver age 75 born in
North Carolina and Sarah age 35 born in Tennessee lived together.
Willis Oliver age 43 whose family consisted of Banetta age 36,
Phebe age 18, Betsy age 7, were in the neighborhood. Then
there was Rhesor Oliver age 55 with a family, including Elvira
age 44, Minerva Ann age 16, Sarah 14, Moses 7, Mary Ellen 4.

Next door to the last mentioned Oliver family lived
Alfred Oliver , a young man age 29 with a very young family.

Also in this district lived the families of Wm.
M. Williams, James Williams, and Dillard P. Williams.

Redding Cooper made his home in this district in
1850. He was born in North Carolina about 1817/8 according
to the 1850 census which gives his age then as 32 years.
His wife was named Elizabeth age 30 a native of Indiana.
Their children are shown as - David C. 10, Frances Mc.9,
Wm.H. 7, James M. 5, Thomas J. 3, Rebecca E. 2, and Mary
E. age one month, all born in Tennessee. In this home also
resided Samuel Fowler age 22 a native of Tennessee.

Next door to them in 1850 resided the family of Core
Cooper age 30 born North Carolina with Elizabeth age 34,
Anthony age 9, Barbara age 6, Kingon age 5, Jacob D, age 2,
and Thomas R age 6 months all born in Tennessee.

Probably the most influential and wealthiest man
in Henry County in 1850 was Terence Cooney, a native of
Virginia. In this year he gave his age as 59. He was a
merchant and reported his property as valued at $18000. In
his home at that time lived Eliza J. age 48 born in
Kentucky. Henrietta age 17, Ellen age 15, James T. age 12,
Charles D. age 10, Henry Clay age 8,Dolly E.H. age 5,
and Wm. Edmunds age 3, all born in Tennessee. Also living
in the family was John Cooney Jr, age 22, a merchant, born
in Tennessee. Cooney and his family were among the earliest
settlers on the Tennessee. The Mouth of Sandy where their
business was established is now a part of Kentucky Lake,
and better known at this date as Paris Landing.

In 1850, next door resided James T. Edmunds, a
Kentuckian, also a man of considerable wealth.With him was
his wife Catherine.

The Cooneys, the Edmunds, some of the Williams and
some of the Courts of Henry County intermarried.

The Cooney family has descendants of that name
residing in Davidson County, Tennessee, at this date,1967.

Robert A.Foster and family. were in the same
vicinity.

Reuben Turpin, the Ferryman, and Ben F. Kendall,
a clerk, also resided there. They worked for Cooney at
one time.

In the Sixteenth Civil District we find John
Kendall the Blacksmith; John F. Kendall, the Shoemaker,
D. Jarrett Kendall, Wm. Kendall, and Eli Kendall and their
families resided.

Hamilton Foster and Thomas Rumbley, some of the
Williams, the Lees, the Thomases, The Neaces (Neeses),

and their families resided.

In this district also resided Jennings H. Courts, a native of Virginia who in 1850 gave his age as 51 years. His family included Eliza G. age 47 born N.C; George W. age 25, Mary A.E. age 21, Susan M. age 16, James A. age 13, William H. age 11, Sarah age 10, Annis age 10, and Mary age 7, all born in Tennessee. This was was closely related to the family of Nathan (Nathaniel) Williams family. They had first settled in Rutherford County, Tennessee after leaving North Carolina, but did not remain there long until the moved to Henry County, where Williams had vast business interests. This family also intermarried with the Cooney family.

Dr. George C. Williams made this district his home.

The Seventeenth Civil District was the home of Phineas Glover, a Virginian, who was born about 1800. He was one of the wealthiest men in the county. In 1850 his estate was listed as having a value of $1000.00 a rather nice sum for that period for any man to have. His wife was Frances a native of North Carolina and was one year older than her husband, according to the census. In 1850 their family consisted of Delilah age 23, Jesse age 22, Martha age 15, and William age 17, all born in Tennessee, indicating that they came to this state at a very early date.

Dr. Josiah H. Porter lived in the seventeenth district. He was a young man in 1850 only 25 years old. His wife Judith was only 21. They had only one child at that time named Ellen age one year.

John C. Porter and family also lived in this district in 1850.

The two most outstanding families in the eighteenth Civil District in 1850 were the Alexanders and the Olivers. Randolph Alexander a South Carolinian born about 1802/3 came to Tennessee before he married. His wife was Elizabeth, a native of the Volunteer State born about 1814. Their children were James 21, John 19, Jonathan 16, Mary 14, Malinda 11, Elizabeth 9, Joseph 6, Deverreaux(?) 4 all born in Tennessee.

Moses Oliver had a large family. He was born in this state 1806/7. He was a Blacksmith, a trade in that day producing a good income. Elizabeth, his wife, was a native of North Carolina, and was born about 1805. Their children were all born in Tennessee according to the census of 1850, namely; John W.,20, James M. 17, Alfred 15, Moses M.13, Victoria 10, Francis M.,8, and Newton M. 5. Andrew J. Clark aged about 35 resided in the home of the Glovers. He was a carpenter.

** * * * * * **

113

INDEX

****

www.ingramcontent.com/pod-product-compliance
Lightning Source LLC
Chambersburg PA
CBHW071135280326
41935CB00010B/1234